How to Find Your Ideal Job in a New Country

A Detailed Guide for International Students

A "how-to" guide and resource for international students, newcomers, and those who need a system for finding their ideal job.

I believe everyone has something special;
That everyone's potential can be realized.
I believe in possibility.
I believe in you!

JoAnne Marlow

How to Find Your Ideal Job in a New Country Copyright © 2023 by JoAnne Marlow.

All rights reserved. No part of this publication may be reproduced, distributed or transmitted in any form or by any means, including photocopying, recording, or other electronic or mechanical methods, without the prior written permission of the publisher, except in the case of brief quotations embodied in critical reviews and certain other noncommercial uses permitted by copyright law.

Although the author and publisher have made every effort to ensure that the information in this book was correct at press time, the author and publisher do not assume and hereby disclaim any liability to any party for any loss, damage, or disruption caused by errors or omissions, whether such errors or omissions result from negligence, accident, or any other cause.

Disclaimer: This book is designed to provide general information for the reader. It is sold with the understanding that the publisher is not engaged to render any type of legal, business or any other kind of professional advice. The content of each chapter is the sole expression and opinion of the author, and not necessarily that of the publisher. No warranties or guarantees are expressed or implied by the publisher's choice to include any of the content in this volume. Neither the publisher nor the author shall be liable for any physical, psychological, emotional, financial, or commercial damages, including, but not limited to, special, incidental, consequential or other damages. The reader is responsible for their own choices, actions, and results. Ms. Marlow's recommendations of books and other resources do not generate any financial gain. Her purpose is strictly to offer these resources to help others.

Published by Prominence Publishing: https://www.prominencepublishing.com

The author can be reached as follows: http://www.joannemarlow.com.

Cover design by Prominence Publishing.

How to Find Your Ideal Job in a New Country/JoAnne Marlow -- 1st ed.

ISBN: 978-1-990830-32-7

Dedication

I wish to thank my family, who always
supports my endeavours to share my wisdom.

You are always there for me, cheering me on,
giving me new ideas and listening to my grandiose visions.

Jaime and Meego Ward-Yassin

Bryan and Shannon Ward

James and Cynthia Marlow

Ashley Marlow

Acknowledgements With Gratitude

Without the hundreds of colleagues, international and Canadian students and friends, who have been willing to share their stories, fears, and ideas to help make this book a "living" success, I would not have written it as it is. I am so proud to be able to thank them for their encouragement, comments, and praise. For these people, I am grateful. Thank you for everything you have done by answering surveys, being interviewed, offering suggestions, helping with research, and cheering me on to complete this vision to help so many new arrivals. The people who need to be thanked are listed on the next pages.

Abdul Qureshi	Batuhan Ozer	Ching Hsiang Tung
Abdullah Shaikh	Berk Kosar	Chloe An
Addie Qiu	Bernadita Balungcas	Chloe Nguyen
Alan Phan	Bernardo Sauza	Chloe Thanh
Alan Tang	Bich Ngoc Nguyen	Chris Fan
Alejandro Hernandez	Brian Gou	Christian Rey Llanto
Alejandro Maciel	Brian Tong	Christina Park
Alexis Andrea Zapanta	Bryan Ward	Chuanzhen Sun
Amritpal Singh	Busra Unal	Chung Liang Cheng
Andrea Villacillo	Canadian Assoc. of Professional Speakers	Damandeep Kaur
Angelica Arenas		Damla Hazal Gurer
Angelica Roque	Cara Lai	Daniel Diaz
Anmoljit Kaur	Carl Suriga	Daniel Robles
Aranveer Sahota	Carla Valenzuela	Daniela Jimenez
Aras Mustafa	Carol Omlang	Darren Zanoria
Ariadne Advincula	Cathrina Sarmiento	Daryl Querijero
Arisbeth Altamirano	Cenk Karakuz	Daryl Santos
Atul Bala	Changrong Zhao	Dave Gonzales
Avengail Roxas	Charles Madayag	David Gouthro
Baba Traore	Cheska Marie Blangket	Dhara Patel
Banu Atilla	Cheska Patanao	Di Yao
Baran Ozturk	Ceyda Gultan	Diana Chavez

Dianne Yabes
Didem Caglar
Dong Chen
Edgar Medrano
Edward Castro
Elaine Lisondra
Elizabeth Acosta
Elizabeth Bonner
Emre Orhan
Erika Flores
Erxin Yan
Eva Rizo
Evelyn Robles
Ezra Tero
Fang Yang
Fehmida Khaki
Finn Cao
Fiona Ran
Francisco Sanchez
Frank Xing
Freda Liu
Fuad Suleymanov
Furkan Ayan
Gagandeep Kaur
German Aguilera
Gilsan Fontanoza
Gurchetan Singh
Gurleen Kaur
Gurleen Singh
Gurpreet Kaur Saini
Gurpreet Singh
Haipeng Yan
Han Wei
Hanul Park
Harjeet Singh
Harman Kaur
Harmandeep Gill
Harmanpreet Singh
Hasan Qureshi
Hazel Mendoza

Heather Walker
Henry Mai
Himanshu Dawar
Hirad Razani
Hyejin Son
Isabel Beltran
Isabel Chan
Isha Devi
Iskender Pehlivan
Ivy Laus Flores
Ivy Mae Comiling
Jackie Bui
Jackie Bunagan
Jacob Divinagracia
Jaemin Cheon
Jagriti
Jaime Ward-Yassin
Jairo Mones
Jane Pan
Janett Garcia
Janice Adlaon
Janice Diongco
Jasdish Baidwan
Jashanpreet Malhi
Jaskaran
Jasmandeep Singh
Jaymarie Vallejo
Jeferson Zuniga
Jenna Pham
Jenyflor Pisco
Jerwin Dublin
Jessica Joy Paguia
Jessie Lam
Jessie Wang
Jeyhun Suleymanov
Ji Shen
Jiaming Zhang
Jiani Long
Jianming Huang
Jiaqi Li

Jiayan Duan
Jiayi Gou
Jihye Shin
Jisu Won
Jiwanjot Singh
Joanna Wan
Joanne Kim
Joanne Tong
John Ilagan
John Rex Rodriguez
Joni David
Joni Ceniza
Jooyoun Kim
Ju Yeon Lee
Juan (Jessica) Zhang
Maria Baeza Beltran
Mati Garcia
Mohit Dadwal
Mohit Verma
Monika
Montserrat Ortega
Murat Ozdayi
Muskan
Muskan Chawla
Naho Takahashi
Namrata
Namrata Maity
Namrata Sood
Natasha Mahusen
Navdeep Kambo
Nikhil Kumar
Nishanth Garimilla
Noah Wang
Omed Husen
Orhan Arslan
Oscar Huang
Oznur Ozbil
Pablo Israel Bano
Pablo Morales Ortiz
Pablo Sevilla

Param Singh	Sarah Alcantara	Warren D'Souza
Pardeep Singh	Saranpreet Kaur	Wei Jin
Parminder Singh	Seren Kos	Wei Liu
Parul	Seungman Lee (Peter)	Weihao Han
Paula Mendoza	Sevval Bekar	Winnie Huang
Pauline Blachford	Shagun Mahajan	Xaverine Ambi
Peiyi Zhu	Shanlei Sood	Xiangxi Yu
Peter Vo	Shanlei Su	Xiaoyu Liu
Pin Chieh Tseng	Sheng Kai Wang	Xie Ping
Ping Xie (Frank)	Shihao Guo	Xin Zhang
Pinghai (Jennifer) Ruan	Shikhu	Xinfang Wang
Pranav Leekha	Simona	Xinyi Liu
Princess Armonio	Sophie Pan	Xinyu Su
Princess Facinabao	Sourav Rai	Xuanyi Wang
Pushpwant Brar	Stella Nguyen	Xuecheng Wang
Qiyang Yu	Steve Barker	Xuehan Yang
Queenie Mangahas	Stephen Esmenda Jr.	Yan Wang
Quyen Truong	Su Im Yoon	Yani Li
Rabia Bano	Sudiksha	Yasak Sogy Verma
Rajdeep Kaur	Sukhpreet Kaur	Yashdeep Kaur
Rajpreet Singh	Sukrucan Tuzgen	Yasser Siddiqe
Rajvinder Kaur	Taha Keskin	Yenchieh Lai
Ramandeep Kaur	Tamara Dracina	Yifei He
Regina Trazona	Tasha Anna Butorac	Yihsuan Lee
Rene Malto Del Ayre	Tatiana David Reyes	Yimeng Li
Rishab Bhoopal	Taylor Zhang	Yoon Jung Lee
River Hernandez	Teresa Diane Bungabong	Yoshiaki Fujita
Riya Dabas		Yu Yang
Rodolfo Tapia	Teresa Robie Bantillo	Yudong Feng
Rodrigo Fierro	Terry Zhou	Yue Qin
Rohit Singh	Thinh Duc Nguyen	Yu Lin Chiu
Romulo Alpas III	Thu Trang Thi Nguyen	Yunlong Fang
Ronald Carl Sebastian	Thu Uyen Bui	Yutong Liu
Roumer Solis Bano	Tom Xu	Yuvraj Igarashi
Roxanne Lambino	Tracy Mai	
Rushikesh Patel	Tsuguru Yamaguchi	
Saleshe Jamilo	Valeria Avalos Taylor	
Samrat	Vanessa Medenilla	
Saninder Thind	Vanessa Ruiz Quiroz	
Sanjna Rani	Vidhi Viradia	

Resulting Praise From My Former Students and Supportive Colleagues

"This book is an exceptional and invaluable resource that offers a wealth of examples and comprehensive instructions to guide international students in pursuing careers that align with their values. What sets this book apart is its remarkable practicality, as even someone like myself, who immigrated to Canada two decades ago, has found relevance within its pages. I wholeheartedly endorse and recommend this book to anyone navigating the job market, as it serves as an empowering tool in discovering and securing meaningful careers."

Jane Pan, MBA
Manager, Centre for Educational Excellence
Simon Fraser University

"This book is a go-to guide for international students and immigrants looking for a meaningful job in their new country. The content is relevant, and I loved the different styles of résumés, offering the readers many options. You encourage your readers to be proactive, thoughtful, and curious about the whole transitioning and hiring process in North American countries. I think this book is excellent!"

Ceyda Gultan
Leadership Coach and HR Consultant

"This book provides a step-by-step guide to navigating the job search process in a new country. It includes practical tips and advice on cultural differences, networking, creating a winning résumé and cover letter, job applications, interviews, and more. As an international student struggling to find a job in a new country or unsure how to approach the job search process, this book will be a useful resource to provide guidance and support for getting an ideal job."

Cenk Karakuz
Resource Management Leader
International Student Graduate

"JoAnne Marlow has created an incredibly valuable reference that gives anyone new to Canada a much better chance of finding the work they really deserve and will enjoy! Written in a conversational tone and sprinkled with her experience, JoAnne provides dozens of credible tips, tools, techniques and references that should assist any newcomer in their search for gainful employment. Every suggestion has an example of what it looks like in practice, making the ideas much more accessible and, dare I say, inspiring! If I had one hope for this book, it would be translated into many different languages—perhaps helping potential newcomers get off to a great start before they even arrive in Canada!"

David Gouthro
Professional Facilitator, Emcee and Meeting Host

"This is the book I needed when I first moved to Canada. This unique, inspiring book will help you find the right path to reach your career."

Mehrak Niroumand
International University Graduate

"As your former student, I am not surprised you have added one more amazing book to your impressive list of accomplishments. Your book is a testament to your expertise in the field and ability to distill complex concepts into accessible language that anyone can understand. I particularly appreciated how you blended theory with real-life examples, making it easy for readers to see the practical applications of the ideas and helpful information you presented.

I have no doubt that your book will become a valuable resource for students and professionals and will be read and referenced for years to come. Your commitment to advancing knowledge in your field is truly inspiring, and I feel incredibly lucky to have had the opportunity to learn from you during my time as your student. Thank you for everything you do, and congratulations again on this wonderful book!"

Jeyhun Suleymanov
International Student Graduate

"When I first met JoAnne, she was a new member of our professional association, CPHR BC, albeit not new to the human resources field. As I became more familiar with JoAnne's portfolio of work, I quickly discovered that the depth and breadth of her expertise were well-suited to a more diverse audience. This included the expanding immigrant talent migration to Canada and the international students choosing to come to BC because our universities are consistently among the top-ranked in Canada. Our highly integrated education system is a global model for progressive, flexible education.

That said, integration has proven to be problematic for many newcomers. A lack of knowledge about Canadian culture, the requisite 'Canadian experience,' and other information relevant to the local workplace culture can make this even more daunting for many new to our small corner of the world. JoAnne has a knack for drilling down to the 'essential,' 'need-to-know' basics that provide a 'how to navigate' this new world, new venture. This is a practical guide for newcomers to Canada. It is full of useful tips, tools, and templates. I highly recommend this book to anyone choosing to come live, work, and play in Canada (or the USA)!"

Elizabeth Bonner
Human Resources Specialist, Non-profit Management
People – Programs – Operations

"When I first opened your book, I was amazed by the extensive content you covered. It will be valuable for international students, and I wish I had read it before coming to Canada as I would have been more prepared. One of my favourite chapters is "Understanding the new job market" because it is the introduction to the rest of the chapters: exploring your options, how to search and accept the right job, decide if it's worth staying or not, among others. That is a crucial chapter where we will understand that we must change our mindsets and adapt to a new country and market.

All the things we have to consider and take care of when moving to a new country are overwhelming, and an excellent example of this is the great list you just made in your chapters. We have to adapt and learn in this new environment constantly. The challenges come in different sizes, and some seem impossible. This book would definitely help international students or people trying to succeed in Canada. Thank you so much for all your effort and your big heart."

Vanessa Ruiz,
International Student

"You have taught me so much as my professor, not only in class but also in life. I will always remember the advice you gave me from this book. I am grateful for you teaching me about finding my ideal job. I was offered a position at the Vancouver Aquarium and signed a contract with them."

Kristine Hidalgosy
International Student

"This book is a comprehensive guide on how to get a job in a new country. It will be extra helpful for new immigrants and definitely be a great resource for career development. JoAnne truly shows her passion in what she does!"

Paula Mendoza,
HR Professional, CPHR recruiter

"This book is an amazing resource for job hunters and those seeking to optimize their career path. It is comprehensive and provides excellent how-to steps to achieve your employment and career goals. Those readers seeking to benefit from this material should seriously take the approaches, detail, and specificity of the instructions and process the author recommends. This book is a unique resource that goes beyond typical job hunting strategies."

James R. F. Marlow, Esq., BASc, CM&AA®, CFP® (Ret.),
MSc, MDR, MBA, JD
President, The Malibu Management Group LLC; CEO,
CFO Management and Dispute Resolution Services

TABLE OF CONTENTS

Introduction 1

Chapter One: Preparing for the Move to a New Country 3

Chapter Two: Understanding the New Job Market 17

Chapter Three: Planning for Your Ideal Career 31

Chapter Four: What's Next? 39

Chapter Five: Setting the Stage for Employment 45

Chapter Six: Writing the Résumé 75

Chapter Seven: Cover Letters and Follow-Up Letters 99

Chapter Eight: Application Forms 127

Chapter Nine: Dropping Off Your Résumé In Person 129

Chapter Ten: Woo Hoo! You've Got an Interview! 133

Chapter Eleven: Dressing for Interview Success 147

Chapter Twelve: Putting it All Together 157

Chapter Thirteen: How to 'Wow' Them with Your
    Interview Skills! 163

Chapter Fourteen: Salary Negotiation 179

Chapter Fifteen: First Day on the Job 189

Chapter Sixteen: Building a Career Path 197

Chapter Seventeen: Navigating Career Challenges 201

Chapter Eighteen: What I Know for Certain… You Will
    Be Successful 211

The Author 215

INTRODUCTION

"Eight out of ten employees are unhappy in their jobs."

~ *JoAnne Marlow*

The statistic above has stayed almost the same for decades. According to Gallup, 2020, only 20% of the world's employees are engaged at work. The rest are "putting up" with boredom, poor management, or other employees who don't share their work ethics or values. At the early age of 22, I made this issue my *purpose:* to enlighten people (students and adults) on what they truly wanted in a career based on their hopes, skills, strengths, and values. As a professional speaker, I have spoken to large and small business senior managers, associations, leaders, governments, Human Resources managers, and individuals on how to hire the best people for their available jobs and create a culture where people are happy to stay longer. As an educator, I have taught thousands of students from Canada and other parts of the world to identify their strengths, skills, and values to eventually align with organizations that value candidates who are talented, excited, and willing to do what it takes to be successfully employed and appreciated.

The value of finding an ideal job that aligns with an individual's strengths, skills, values, work ethics, and future plans is the difference between working in a career that brings you joy and fulfillment for years and one that may bring frustration, misery and short-term employment.

I have learned so much, having experienced happiness and frustration in my career choices. Being a constant researcher, I know the tips, tools, templates and links I offer in this book will give you an "edge" and better prepare you to find and accept that ideal job. I wish to help you transition easily to your new country and prepare yourself to find what will make you happy you came here rather than leaving you frustrated and discouraged.

Along with this book, you will find several references to a landing page and additional links to resources, information and templates to download. The data will be updated regularly when new information is available.

The website landing page is
http://www.joannemarlow.com/employmentguide

This book prepares you for success as you transition to a new life in a new country.

Chapter One

PREPARING FOR THE MOVE TO A NEW COUNTRY

Let's get something totally clear. I am writing this book because I respect you and want to help you with the changes you will face. When a person decides to leave their family, home and country for any reason…for freedom, a potentially better life, a North American education, or just for the experience, I am in awe of you. I genuinely respect you for the sacrifices you are making to have a new life and the courage to leave everything you may love to come to a new country.

It can be an exciting yet scary opportunity for many people who come to Canada, the USA, or any new country for their education. Many come to live, study and eventually receive their Permanent Residency (PR) card with the hopes of creating a better life. Given the promise of those situations, you still need to support yourself (and your family) while you adjust to a new country, its diverse population and cultures. And, of course, you must practice a new language – English.

When you arrive, everything will be new to you. The environment, housing, transportation, people, shopping, communication and learning methods are only a few changes you will experience. It will be a challenge, and I know you can do it.

My Short Story

As a young graduate entering the workforce, my challenge wasn't the language. I was born in Canada and only learned English. My challenge was "equality," or the lack of it, where women were not considered for jobs in business other than as secretaries. My interest was in business management, and at university, I was challenged in my class which was mostly made up of men. When I took a career and personality assessment at the university, the female psychologist called me a "masculine female." That comment had a profound effect on who I became as well as my future choices. Back in the day, I had to work harder than most men in my class, as I was only one of four women in my class of almost 90 students studying economics and commerce. After graduating, my interviews were insulting to my gender.

I was asked whether I was in a serious relationship, indicating that I wouldn't be of value to the company if I were to get married and have children. To the recruiter's surprise, I had done my research and learned that over 80% of my class expected to stay at their first job for a maximum of two years. I mentioned that statistic to the interviewers. I told them that marriage and having children would not affect my ability to work if I were properly matched with a company that valued my worth. I stood up, shook hands, thanked them for their time and left. This treatment was repeated several times, and I became very frustrated. I returned to university to get my teaching degree, and even then, I was the only person with a business degree who wanted to teach business. However, little did I know that teaching what I loved (business and leadership) would be my "ideal" career choice. Thank goodness some things have changed in the past several decades. However, some business employers still have old-fashioned and inappropriate views on whom they should hire.

The content in this book will give you some knowledge and suggestions to work on yourself and your confidence and to determine how to present your best, defined self for the life of happiness you deserve. I hope you are more prepared to transition to your new world before leaving your country.

Your Potential Challenges

One of the several surprises you will face due to immigration laws is that you may be extremely limited in the positions you are allowed to fill. Many of you may already have university degrees from your home country, and you could be disappointed as many of your degrees will not be recognized in Canada. These rules come from the federal government, universities, and policies and guidelines from professional associations. You can learn more about the laws from the various links I've supplied to help you as you transition to your new country. The following link will be regularly updated to provide information, links, and education to more sites to help you: www.joannemarlow.com/employmentguide

Many people are concerned about finding work when they arrive. If you are still deciding on a university, read the information provided by your learning institution and the Immigration rules and procedures for new arrivals from the Internet. Note that the Immigration laws are different in Canada from the USA, and no assumptions of similarity should be made. Make sure you understand the restrictions before you arrive. There is a process for hiring in your new country that will likely be quite different from what you are used to. Sadly, there is no preferential treatment for new arrivals, as you must compete with all the others seeking work. The hiring procedures are the same, no matter where you were born. Employers seek people with good attitudes, skills, and efficiency to help them build their businesses. They will do their best to accommodate your available hours. Still, since your classes at university change from term to term, your employer must understand that flexibility is needed for you to be your best as you study and work. This may be challenging, and some people might need two part-time jobs to work around their availability.

Feeling Overwhelmed and Unsupported

If you are travelling on your own, it can be natural to feel alone and nervous. I know this to be true. It would be best to take care of several things before and certainly, when you arrive—finding a place to stay, seeing your immigration agent, shopping, learning the transportation system and attending the campus, where you will meet many strangers…who feel just like you! The main thing to remember is that you will find excellent support from the university staff, and the people there will give you more information as you make friends.

In one of the last chapters, I will discuss some ideas to consider if you feel your mental health, confidence, or fears are starting to take over.

You Already Have Valuable Skills for Employment

The good news is that most businesses welcome international students to their workplaces. Canada and the USA have an abundance of new arrivals from around the world, and many are seeking education and jobs, just like you. You are certainly not alone in your quest. The good news is that you may surprise yourself with the multitude of skills that you have already developed throughout your life. Regardless of your previous work, you must realize that you already have employability skills and excellent transferable or soft skills that apply to many positions. Transferable skills are non-technical abilities and skills that depend on traits and characteristics such as emotional intelligence, values and work ethics. These talents largely depend on the person's innate (born-with) beliefs about accountability and respect. Organizations value candidates with strong, soft skills because they typically work well in teams and collaboration, which adds to a positive organizational culture. Many of these soft skills have been learned, experienced, or are part of your personality. They are important and valuable employable skills. Check the following list of some highly valued transferable skills. Perhaps highlight or create a list of the ones that you have.

These may include:

Ability to work with a team	Healthy work-life balance
Adaptability	Humility
Analytical skills	Kindness
Attention to detail	Languages
Collaboration	Leadership
Communication	Management
Computer knowledge	Organization
Conflict resolution	Polite, well-mannered
Creative expression	Problem-solving
Creativity	Project management
Critical thinking	Punctual
Customer service	Research
Dependability	Selflessness
Empathy	Strong work ethics
Flexibility	Teamwork
Friendliness	Technical skills
Hardworking	Time management

Trustworthy   Writing

Transferable and soft skills are appreciated and are worthy of putting on your résumé, no matter where you live. You will learn additional technical and soft skills after earning a new position.

Student Work Permit

An international student work permit allows students to work several hours each week while attending school, and in Canada, the number of hours has recently changed from 20 to 40 hours per week. You can work up to 40 hours per week in a job off the campus grounds (i.e., in the community). This option is in place until December 31, 2023, and if that rule extends or changes, you can still work full-time during official school breaks, such as the winter and summer holidays or term breaks or after you finish your studies and apply for a non-student work permit.

Of course, you do not need to work while you attend school; however, obtaining Canadian or North American experience (volunteer or paid work experience) is crucial in being considered for more responsible positions later. Volunteering or working part-time or full-time can show you have several months or years of work experience in your new country. As mentioned earlier, the tricky thing is finding employers who can be flexible with your education timetable. The other challenge is that no matter what degrees or experience you bring from your home country, you are only eligible to apply for entry-level positions. You can search for potential jobs here: (https://www.canadim.com/guides/noc-codes).

This is a Canadian Immigration regulation. This site explains the TEER system. The TEER (Temporary Employment Exemption Regulations) system is a program that allows international students in

Canada to work off-campus without a work permit. The TEER program replaced the previous system known as the NOC (National Occupational Classification) program, which required international students to find a job related to their field of study and obtain a work permit before they could work off-campus. To be eligible for the TEER program, international students must be enrolled in a full-time program of study at a designated learning institution (DLI) in Canada. They must also have a valid study permit and be in good academic standing. The main restriction is that you are prohibited from working in jobs considered dangerous or harmful to public health and safety.

Employers and governments must ensure that your learned skills from other countries are equal and equivalent to our country's laws, rules, and skills for some professions (e.g., public educators are certified to teach in one Canadian province only. The educator must acquire new training to teach in other provinces or countries). Each province (or state) has their own government rules that they obey. However, you can work anywhere if you have apprenticed or have earned a Journeyman's ticket. There are over 100 trades in Canada and the USA, and skilled workers are in high demand (and are paid well, while training as an apprentice).

After you find a job, have proven your skill level, and acquired the employer's trust that you can do the job well and demonstrate you can take on more responsibilities, your position may change, or you can search for more challenging work. The critical thing to remember is that you are entitled to work in Canada or another country, should be treated with respect, and obtain training from your new employer. If they are unwilling to offer these, either **don't** take the job or start looking for something elsewhere. Asking about the available training during an interview will help you determine if this is the best job for you. You deserve to be treated with respect and be trained well.

As a Senior Associate faculty member at a university in Vancouver, British Columbia, that offers degrees for international students, I am concerned that many students may have to work several part-time jobs or work late on occasion. This can create a hardship after attending up to eight hours of classes per day occasionally. Remember that your health is essential for both your education and employment productivity. Start searching and potentially applying for jobs before you leave your country. Speak to friends, alum members from the university, or the university's student services. You may also choose remote or contract jobs (where you can work from home) with flexible hours and days. Many students continue their online businesses from their home country to supplement their income. However, employers will always ask if you have experience in your new country before they hire you.

Are You the Right Fit?

Looking for work is the easy part of getting a job. The hard part is preparing for a position that will excite you, match your skills, motivation and values, and get an interview. There is a massive labour shortage in Canada and the USA, and employers are eager to find the "right fit." Undoubtedly, there are differences in the job application processes between your country and North America. We cover this in the following chapters.

Today, it's rare for someone to spend their entire career doing the same job at the same place. People may go to college or university to train for one particular job but often end up doing various jobs throughout their lives. However, as you change jobs, you will use and build on similar skills and strengths in different positions.

As you transition from a previous job or life, you will gain new skills and determine your likes and dislikes. Whether your position is temporary in your mind, doing your best at each job, no matter how humble it may seem, will reap the rewards of gaining references from your employers and help you gain the new country experience you need.

Remember, if you change from one job to another, where you only spend a few months at a job, future employers will wonder if you are reliable for the long term. It costs the employer an average of $14,000 to replace a minimum wage employee in British Columbia, Canada and for the new hire to reach the same productivity level. (The minimum wage in BC is currently $16.75 per hour). The employer must be convinced that you are choosing the right job and that the position meets your interests, personality, and skills. To them, this would mean you may stay there longer. Taking "any old job" to earn money quickly could lead to what some call a "Day Prison." This is where a person accepts a job or environment that proves unpleasant. Sadly, some people can't afford to leave because this is their only source of income. Later, I will discuss why you do NOT need to accept this type of life. There is a better way.

As I mentioned earlier, eight out of ten workers are unhappy in their jobs. This shocking and sad statistic helped me realize my purpose in life. I couldn't believe why people would not only take a job that was not providing some value and purpose

> *Working in a position where there is an alignment with your skills, strengths, and values is critical if you and the employer are both satisfied.*

in their lives or why they would "settle" for a less rewarding job. I have spent my adult life working with youth and adults of all ages and positions to determine what type of jobs or careers align with their skills, strengths, and values. Once a person identifies "their why" or purpose and what will bring them the most joy, the job search is more focused, and they can identify an employer who will be the best match for them. I now work with business owners and human resource managers to help them hire employees better aligned with the organization's vision, values and culture. Slowly but surely, employees and businesses find the right talent who believe in the organization's vision and purpose. Employees can move forward with a career path instead of seeking another job elsewhere, hoping for a better fit. Knowing your purpose is critical if you and your employer are both to be satisfied. I cannot emphasize this last statement enough. And, you have just as much right to ask the employer questions during the interview as they do to determine whether you are a good fit for the position. In a later chapter, there are more details on how to define your purpose in life.

Learning English - Yes, it is Necessary

Don't assume that your English comprehension and speaking ability are satisfactory for most Canadian businesses. That statement was difficult for me to say, as I admire you so much for the sacrifices you are making to leave your country and move far away for what you hope is a better life. Writing and speaking English is difficult for anyone, even if it is their first language, and I applaud your desire to learn and speak it. I assume most students already have some basic English from their countries, courses online, or TOEFL classes in their new country. There are free practice TOEFL tests online, as well. In addition to attending extra English classes, here are some tips to help you improve your English vocabulary and pronunciation. You will notice a significant improvement in your English vocabulary and communication when you work at it.

- Listen to English-speaking television, movies, YouTube Ted-X presentations, and radio programs.

- Become a friend with an English-speaking person. You may meet them on the bus, in class, or at a coffee shop. You will have to speak English.

- Learn to sing some English songs and what they mean.

- Read aloud or to someone in your family so you can hear your English pronunciation.

- Enrol in a free English language course in person or online. (E.g., Duolingo.com or Babbel.com)

- *Slow down* when you speak English. This will allow you the time to say the words correctly and pronounce each syllable. Others will be able to understand you, despite your accent. The average speed of the English language is between 160 – 190 words per minute. If you traditionally speak languages from China, India, Mexico, the Middle East or South Asia, the typical speed of your speech may be upwards of 500 words per minute. Employers and others will appreciate you speaking more slowly.

- Ask your English-speaking friends and instructors to correct your pronunciation if needed.

- Sign in to Grammarly.com (Premium) to improve your grammar, spelling, punctuation and sentence structure for all your essays, emails, cover letters and résumés. When you pay for a year's subscription, you can get a significant discount for the following year. Your instructors will thank you, as well! And as a university instructor, I found that the student's grammar improved so much, as well as their learning. Their marks increased due to paying attention to the corrections suggested by Grammarly. Just so you know, the Grammarly app will offer choices allowing you to decide which words to use to improve your grammar, spelling, punctuation and sentence clarity.

- Speak only English when you are chatting with friends and family. Practice will make you a better communicator. Speak English in school and classrooms. It is tempting to speak your native language with others, but you won't improve your English that way.

- To improve your English grammar, you can visit several **free sites** to help you learn. www.KhanAcademy.org is an excellent non-profit organization allowing you to start anywhere in your understanding (beginner to advanced) and help you progress. It is an online program with an instructor, lessons and quizzes. As you improve, your confidence will improve. Apps such as Duolingo.com (offers free and paid versions) and Babbel.com (paid version) are good sites to explore for learning another language. Both will help you with vocabulary, but Babbel offers a short lesson and deals with grammar as well, while Duolingo is more focused on vocabulary and is more of a game. The paid versions of either App are between $6 -$10 US/month, based on the current price at this time of writing. You can review a clear comparison at this site:

https://testprepinsight.com/comparisons/babbel-vs-duolingo/

Chapter Two

UNDERSTANDING THE NEW JOB MARKET

Depending on the industry, location and current economic conditions, the job market in your new country varies. Most of Canada's population sits about 100 km north of the American border. The largest populations are in Toronto, Ontario; Montreal, Quebec; Vancouver, British Columbia and Calgary, Alberta. However, there are colleges and universities in northern cities, where the cost of living is usually less than in highly populated areas. As a warning, you may often deal with more intense winter conditions in northern environments. Over the past ten years, I've noticed that our weather patterns in Canada are changing. Vancouver, BC, where I live, typically has milder temperatures year-round. Being on the Pacific Ocean and in a mountain range, we usually get a lot of rain. However, over the past five years, we've had less rain and some snow, and our summers have been much hotter and dryer. It's a good idea to check the weather patterns of your intended location to see if you can deal with the weather compared to where you are from. Nonetheless, business continues regardless of the weather. Getting to school or work should rarely be a transportation issue.

First, you must be authorized to work in the country without restrictions. Applying to a university or college will allow you to work part-time while enrolled in an educational institution. Immigration laws often limit the number and, certainly, the types of jobs you can apply for, which may be entry-level jobs, regardless of your previous education or experience. It is disappointing but necessary for you to become accustomed to your new environment, work ethic and expectations within a business in Canada or the US. With a positive attitude and hard work toward the tasks, you will gain the trust of your new employer and will likely be considered for more challenging opportunities. Having patience, although it is difficult, is needed.

Initially, you may find that your spoken English is a barrier to finding work, especially where your spoken and written English is essential. In the previous chapter, I touched on activities to help you improve. It's worth taking a good look at the ideas and taking action.

Many resources are also available to help international students navigate the job market in North America. Many universities and colleges have student career centers that offer career advice, job listings and networking opportunities. International students can take advantage of job fairs, informational interviews and internships to gain valuable work experience and make connections in their field.

Additionally, international students and new arrivals can take advantage of organizations whose purpose is to help you transition into your new country. (e.g., Mosaic BC, in Vancouver). Below are some suggestions for finding out more about job availability, housing, and general market information.

1. **Visit Government Websites:** The Government of Canada provides information on job outlooks, salaries, and employment prospects in different industries. Explore the Employment and Social Development. Canada's Job Bank (https://www.jobbank.gc.ca) an excellent resource for information on job openings, wages, skills, and job profiles required for various occupations.

2. **Check Industry-Specific Websites:** Many industries have associations or organizations that provide information on job opportunities and industry trends. For example, if you are interested in the technology industry, the Information and Communications Technology Council (ICTC) provides information on job prospects, skills, and training requirements. https://www.ictc-ctic.ca/

3. **Utilize Career Centers**: Many Canadian universities and colleges have career centers that offer resources and support for international students seeking employment. More prominent universities and colleges can advise on job search strategies, résumé writing, and interview preparation.

4. **Network:** Networking is an excellent way of finding a job in Canada. Connect with alums, professors, and other professionals in your field through online platforms such as LinkedIn or attend networking events. Building connections can help you learn about job openings and get recommendations. Talk to any relatives or friends you may have living in your destination. They can assist you in finding suitable work and housing.

5. **Seek Help from Immigration Consultants and Agents**: An immigration consultant or agent can assist you in navigating the Canadian job market and help you understand the job qualifications and requirements for your field of interest. They can also advise on the immigration process and assist you in obtaining the necessary work permits.

6. **Go to Several Informational Interviews**: This is one of the best ways to meet people in a job you might consider ideal for you. You will spend about 15-20 minutes with this person, ask them a series of questions and then determine if: a) this might be an excellent job for you in the future, b) you have the qualifications (or interests in gaining the skills) for this position, c) if this is a company you may want to work for someday d) if this is not a good choice for you at any time in your life.

What are the Right Jobs for You?

You will gain a lot of information in this book. This chapter is a good one to read to learn about the available jobs in your new country. When recruiting candidates for clients, I was always surprised at the number of people who applied for a job even though they weren't qualified. Out of 100 applications, it was often difficult to find ten candidates who were qualified for the education, experience, and personality required. It wastes the recruiter's time as they sift through each application. I recommend that if you fully qualify for at least 80% of the requirements, it may be appropriate for you to apply for the job. Many employers can't spare the time to teach you new software or give you a job that requires at least five years of experience. Instead, apply to jobs that seem interesting to you, are related to the industry you want to pursue, and offer some training, but not weeks of training.

When I was recruiting on behalf of my clients, I asked the candidates to supply a résumé and a detailed cover letter to explain why they felt qualified to apply for this job and to complete the two quick tests for typing speed and customer service, as they related to the job duties.

Anyone who missed even one requirement was rejected. The message here is that you must be mindful to complete **all** the steps required by the employer if you want to be considered.

An Interesting Way to Explore the Market

I had no idea what job I wanted when I decided to leave teaching in the public sector, although I was interested in Human Resources. Still, I had so much success helping people gain their confidence, strengths and skills as an educator and District Career Programs Coordinator that I wondered if I might prefer a job helping displaced employees (those terminated due to the economy, performance, or changes in the business ownership). I interviewed twelve business people (all unknown to me) to determine what their jobs were like and to assess if the company and their career were the right one for me. I created the steps below for an "informational interview." I chose people in management roles for large and medium-sized companies. In most cases, based on the script below, I was able to find the ideal person to talk with, and in some cases, the interview lasted anywhere from 20 to 60 minutes. I also asked for referrals, had my résumé assessed, and was offered two jobs. I accepted one.

By taking these steps, international students can better understand the Canadian job market and develop strategies to increase their chances of securing employment in their chosen field.

Informational Interviews

One of the best and most successful ways to network, meet potential employers and research various career fields is through an Informational Interview.

You would "interview" a person in a field or career that may interest you. In addition, you'll learn about the profession, the qualifications needed, and the enjoyable and less-than-enjoyable parts of the job.

Where can you locate these strangers who won't mind talking to you? You can approach a person through a friend, relative or even your immigration agent or through what is termed a "cold call." A cold call is where you contact an employer via phone or LinkedIn. Once the connection is made, you would call to schedule an appointment to "interview" or question them on their career. You are seeking career information, **not** a job interview, so make sure you clarify that.

Purpose or Objectives of the Interview

- You will find out whether or not their career matches your needs, skills and interests. If it is, you will then be able to determine what you need to do to follow that career path (such as skills, education, etc.).

- You can determine the type of new employee the company hires for junior positions (so that you can grow with the company).

- You can inquire whether or not the company is hiring soon.

- You can get a good contact person in the industry to shadow, have as a mentor, a networking contact, or an internship opportunity.

- You can ask for other referred contact names to phone and interview.

- It may be a good opportunity for them to comment on your résumé and give you some valuable feedback.

How to Determine Whom to Contact

I suggest that you consider the types of jobs you're interested in. Do a thorough search on job sites such as Indeed.com, GlassDoor.com, SimplyHired.com, etc. Remember to vary your job titles, as you may come up with various jobs under specific headings. For example, finding the ideal job description for an Organization Development specialist took me a while. I searched under Learning and Development, Leadership Trainer, and Change Management and found different jobs under each category.

Once you have determined the names of the positions that appeal to you, make a note of the companies that are searching for people to hire. Often the website or a phone number is included. However, you can visit the organization's website and get the contact names or business phone numbers there.

Initial Contact

Phone the business. Ask to speak to the person in charge of hiring (in the Human Resources (HR) department). If they block your conversation, saying they are not hiring now, reply that you are not seeking a job.

Let them know you are seeking information about a career that interests you and want to speak with someone in the company with a position in the _____ department. (The blank represents the position title or department name that may interest your curiosity). They may put you through to that department or to HR.

Suggested Phone Script

Be polite. Prepare; have a calendar, a pen, and résumé in front of you.

"Hello, my name is Pablo Mateo. Is Mr. Jones available, please?"

> If the "gatekeeper" answers, "No, (s)he's busy," then ask when it will be a good time to call again. Do not expect them to contact you; they are busy and may not recall your name. You can leave your name and number, but YOU MUST call them back.

"Hello, Mr. Jones; my name is Pablo Mateo. I am studying business and human resources at X University. I was hoping you could spend 15 or 20 minutes with me in the next week or two to answer my questions about the various specialties within your career or department. I am trying to determine if ____ is the right career choice for me and would appreciate hearing the facts from someone in the field."

> They'll respond and may ask you a question... which you can answer.

"I can meet with you on Tuesdays, Wednesdays, or Thursdays. Would one of these days work well for you? Wednesday? That would be great. What time is suitable? Yes, 4:30 is fine."

"Thank you very much, Mr. Jones. I look forward to meeting you on Wednesday, March 12th, at 4:30 in the afternoon. Is your office at 786 Main Street? Perfect. Thank you. Good-bye."

My Experience with Informational Interviews

Here's a routine I used when I attended twelve informational interviews.

- ❏ Research the company and read the interviewer's LinkedIn or Google profiles. That will allow you to become more familiar with a new contact and the company they work for.

- ❏ Dress appropriately for the interview and have a list of questions in a notebook (or journal) and a couple of pens (in case the ink dries). Take two or three résumés with you.

- ❏ Ensure you have clear directions to your destination (by transit or car) and leave ample time for traffic, bad weather, parking or getting lost.

- ❏ Arrive at the business, introduce yourself to the receptionist, and state that you have an appointment with Mr./Ms. Jones

- ❏ Shake hands with Mr./Ms. Jones, and thank them for seeing you. State again that you are a student at X University and trying to determine your best career path. You have some questions prepared and hope that you won't take more than 20 minutes of their time.

- ❏ Open your Journal and open the conversation; start with a general question, such as "What is your professional title? How long have you been in this career?" (Many questions are below, so choose at least ten.) Please take a seat when they direct you to do so.

- ❑ One of the crucial things is to share your résumé with them. As you get your résumé, ask politely if they can glance at it and offer advice. In my experience, only one person declined that suggestion.

- ❑ Keep your eye on the time; you do not want to upset their schedule. Watch for them to do a body shift or glance at their watch to indicate the interview is over.

- ❑ Before you leave, ask if they know anyone who could give another perspective on this career.

Even though you intend to gather valuable information about that career and any possibilities that they may have openings in the future, you may also be open to working there full-time. I was taken by surprise (and delight) when two employers offered me jobs. I was available to take a full-time position at the time, and within two weeks, I was the manager for the education division of a global organization. Remember, I didn't have any management experience in a big company. My business skills were "learned" and not necessarily practiced. I had a lot to learn, and because I "knew" my strengths and weaknesses, I was confident that I would learn and enjoy my new position.

Questions for Informational Interviews

(Typically, you can choose ten questions in a 20-minute interview. You can arrange them based on their importance to you).

1. What is required in your profession? What responsibilities and tasks do you do?

2. How did you become interested in (or aware of) your profession?

3. What interests did you have as a young adult that have helped you in this career?

4. How did you decide what you wanted to do?

5. What educational background do you have?

6. How long does it take to train for your position? How often are the training sessions? Do you still take courses to stay current?

7. What is your typical day like?

8. Do you enjoy going to work, and why?

9. What do you dislike about your work?

10. What has your career path (or working background) been? (Since post-secondary training)

11. What do you see in the future for your profession?

12. What do you look for in a potential employee?

13. What job would a new person have in your field? How fast could they progress?

14. What is the salary (or wage) range for someone starting?

15. What would a first-year employee be learning and doing?

16. How can you determine that a person will make a promising recruit?

17. What is required for your job in terms of the following:

    - Personality and people skills
    - Emotional status and stability
    - Physical ability
    - Intellectual ability

18. How did you know that this was a good occupation for you?

19. Where would I go to school to get training for your profession?

20. What prerequisites are needed for enrollment in the training institution for your profession?

21. What does your job have to offer?

22. Have you considered leaving your profession, and if so, why?

23. What technology is used in your job? And what programs should I learn?

24. What career options are available in your career?

25. Can you go into most businesses with your current skills and training?

26. Would this be a good option considering our economy's state and demographics? (E.G., the population concerning age, gender, socio-economic status, etc.)

After the interview, stand up, and thank the person for their time and information. Shake their hand firmly. Let them know how valuable their information was. Ask for a business card to thank them and properly add them to your connections list. Please offer a couple of your résumés in case one of their colleagues is interested in you as an intern or employee. Follow up with a thank you letter in a card, email, or letter.

Chapter Three

PLANNING FOR YOUR IDEAL CAREER

Explore Your Options

Planning helps you accomplish your goals from beginning to end. It includes outlining your goals, creating strategies, and checking in on your progress and success. Knowing yourself, your attitudes, skills, strengths, behaviours, and weaknesses will help you determine the best career and employer for you and your future.

The Conference Board of Trade (2023) has published a document on the skills required by current employers. You can go to their link and review the current abilities, their meaning and examples and then determine where your strengths lie. They update this list annually. https://www.conferenceboard.ca/future-skills-centre

Know Who You Are

Many international students and new arrivals fear rejection from employers, and that is a realistic fear. There are many things that you may need to learn or understand. You may have left your parents and family behind and feel all alone. There may be no one to guide you or offer advice or support. However, I firmly believe that your confidence and courage will grow when you determine the type of career you want. Afterwards, you can create a path for your jobs and, eventually, a career based on your purpose, strengths, values and best characteristics. Those who know themselves well, regardless of where they are from, are successful, especially when prepared.

Many people, especially those new to Canada or the USA, need to know what jobs are available and what skills the employers seek from international candidates. Before you search for jobs, take the time to understand what you can offer your employer in strengths, skills, values and experience. During the interview, you will be asked specific questions; if you are unprepared, you will struggle with your answers. As a result, you may not get the job you'd love to have. It will help immensely if you are well acquainted with what you can offer an employer.

> Those who know themselves well, regardless of where they are from, are successful, especially when prepared.

Knowing what you value in life, the people you want to work with, the tasks you'll do, and the environments you prefer will help you be more selective about the responsibilities you enjoy. Researching the market and knowing that you will fit in and be valued for your skills and strengths will satisfy you. Isn't that what you want? This is an opportunity to explore what jobs are available in your new location. Many new students are so eager to take "any" job to pay the bills that they are disheartened when that job doesn't satisfy or challenge them to be who they are or could be. Worse than that is staying at a job you dislike, which employees have named "Day Prison."

To fully understand how it feels when working at a job you dislike, you can do this short exercise.

> Write or print (in English) your name on paper. Then, place the pen in your opposite hand and attempt to write your name as well as you did initially.

How did you feel when you changed hands? I'm sure you finished the task but may have needed more concentration or time. Perhaps you were concerned that your second try wouldn't have been acceptable. Some people even became frustrated and wanted to give up. Were you pleased with your second attempt? Or were you worried it wouldn't be good enough?

The lesson from this exercise is that even though you wrote your name using both hands, your emotions, when switching hands, are almost identical to working in a job you dislike. Your productivity is slower; you must concentrate more, and the task can become frustrating or annoying. Can you imagine if you had to write with your weaker hand all the time? It is the same with a job that doesn't fit with who you are. You would not be using your natural strengths. Eventually, you would become unhappy and leave that job, having to start the job search all over again. There is something that you can do about this, however.

People worldwide and of all ages wander aimlessly from job to job because they don't know what career is best for them. The fortunate ones who determine their perfect career feel focused, alive, joyful and fulfilled. I'm often approached by clients who ask me, "How do I figure out my purpose in life?" Sometimes, it is just a statement, a statistic, or a cause that alerts or awakens a person's feelings or passion. It may be something that ignites a spark in your mind. It is difficult for me to explain, as I was only 22 years old when I was moved by a statistic that hit me like a sack of rocks. Earlier, I mentioned that I read a business article stating that eight out of ten employees were unhappy. I honestly couldn't understand why so many people would choose to stay in a job that didn't challenge and excite them. As a new high-school teacher of twelfth-graders, my job was exciting, as I got to share my ideas and lessons with young learning minds each day. I was free to develop my classes and curriculum and was able to share my love of learning with my students. As a result, my purpose was clear: "to help people find careers that would excite and challenge them."

> Today, 30% of those people who are still unhappy in their jobs will not take action to change. How sad.

Over the years, I learned how to help people determine their purpose and locate jobs and employers who would be a good match. A good "match" would be where the employer's values, vision, and purpose would be similar to yours. For decades, I followed my passion by teaching people how to find their purpose and determine their best skills and strengths, leading them to a fulfilling career. I've had the opportunity to influence thousands of young people and adults. Today, I speak professionally to business leaders and human resources managers to help them redefine their purpose and visions and find employees who perfectly match the business's goals.

Without a doubt, many people struggle to find a career or job they enjoy, as they have not determined what they are good at, where they should work, and what will help to fulfill their lives. I don't often suggest that my clients and students purchase books, but I can certainly refer to two books that have significantly impacted peoples' career choices. These books will be one of your best investments to help you find that ideal job or career.

Simon Sinek wrote *"Start with Why"* (2011), one of the most influential books I have ever read that offers a process to find your purpose. This book will take you through the steps to help you determine (or validate) your purpose and direct you toward the jobs or opportunities that will give you the most satisfaction and joy in life. Over a million books have been sold. You can borrow the book from the library, listen to it on Audible, purchase it as a paperback, or digitally download it on Kindle through Amazon or a library. With the knowledge of your purpose, your job search will become more focused, and you'll be more likely to accept only those jobs that meet your purpose.

Having a purpose is like the metaphor of the North Star. Just like the sailors who navigated to places unknown, you can navigate your life. When you get turned around, wander from job to job, and get off course, you can constantly realign yourself by seeking your north star or purpose. It keeps you focused on finding your ideal employer and position. It becomes your compass in life. **You** alone will be in charge of your future.

Have I ever gone off my path? Oh ya! Occasionally, I explored other avenues and careers and eventually realized I had become one of those unhappy statistics. And how did I know? After the novelty of the new job wore off, I became unhappy, grumpy, sick, stressed, slower, and started to complain to my family. It wasn't like I was "writing with the weaker hand," it was more like writing with my foot! Sometimes it took me a while before I decided to leave, but I was relieved when I found a job that aligned with who I was and what

I could happily offer a company. I have never felt more satisfied, happy, and free of 'work.' Instead, my job is a true joy, and I "play" daily. It sounds impossible, right? It's not.

Another metaphor for the importance of knowing your purpose or passion in life is similar to when trying to find a specific or unusual ingredient for your meal. You may seek out other stores if you can't initially locate the ingredient. You may even research the Internet where you can find such an ingredient, as, without it, the recipe you are preparing will not be enjoyable. Again, it is similar to choosing a job that does not relate to your purpose, strengths, values and attributes. A substitute isn't the same and may ruin your chances of enjoying your new position.

The other books I recommend are "Now, Discover Your Strengths" by Marcus Buckingham and Don Clifton (2001) or a similar book, StrengthsFinder 2.0 (2007) by Tom Rath.

ALERT: This book **must** be new, and ensuring that the red envelope at the back is **unopened** is critical. The code inside the envelope is your only access to your Strengths assessment and **can only be used once**. You'll be presented with a series of assessment questions by entering the code from the sealed envelope into the Internet search engine. Once completed and submitted, you'll be emailed a description of your five innate (born-with) strengths. Even though you may scoff at needing to assess your strengths, the words and phrases used to describe your attributes will provide you with the most fantastic vocabulary to use in your résumé, cover letter and interview conversation. People who use this book gain clarity on their identity, and how to apply these strengths significantly boosts their confidence as they will be able to describe how their strengths will be of value to their new position. Out of more than thirty assessments I have sampled, this one has been the most accurate and helpful in helping me land ideal positions using the "right" words. It is worth the price.

Some free assessments are online; however, the ones I sampled don't compare with the detailed and rich descriptions of your strengths. In addition, you'd still need to buy the book to gain more information. If you purchase the book from a store or Amazon, check that the envelope is sealed before you purchase. You may not be able to return the book if the envelope is open (even by someone else)!

Here's an example of a portion of a cover letter for a position as a Learning Development Specialist where I used descriptions versus the descriptive language from the assessment. When I used the phrases from the assessment, I was delighted to be contacted within a week by several employers for an interview. And the most exciting part is that I was offered a position I LOVE.

Before the Assessment

"I love the challenge of determining the core problem. As a Certified Life Coach, I can earn the trust and rapport of senior executives who share their concerns and information willingly.

One of my strengths is my creative problem-solving to develop potential options to resolve the problem. I have found that using my strategies for interventions, whether for individuals, teams or the entire organization, makes sense and allows the transition to be accepted by the employees for longer-lasting change and improved productivity."

After the Assessment

"As a problem solver, I am *innovative, inventive, origina*l, and *resourceful.* I entertain ideas about how to *reach a goal, increase productivity,* or *solve a problem.* First, I *think of alternatives. Then I choose the best option.*

My *personality and energy are upbeat,* and I can *get others excited* about what they will do.

I like to think that through my continuous research, I can *fill the gaps when most people don't even realize there are gaps.* My personality involves *quickly developing rapport and trust* with others. I listen. I care. I *can help them learn and apply their new ideas* and knowledge."

Chapter Four

WHAT'S NEXT?

Know How Much Money You Will Need to Earn

When you come to a new country, everything is different. The money, the cost of living, transportation, grocery stores and entertainment may shock you. Do your research before you leave your home country. Know how much it will cost you to live and attend school. Many students are surprised when more than one part-time job is required and take on late-evening jobs to make ends meet. Without a doubt, you will be exhausted and not have time to complete your assignments and readings on time, and there is a stronger possibility that you will do poorly in your grades. Most English-speaking students take only three courses each term, as the study requirements are time-consuming and often challenging. You are also competing with others for high grades and are often expected to work in teams, where others depend on your contributions and accountability. No human can be highly productive with a lack of time or sleep. Many students must practice time management, prioritizing tasks, and budgeting their finances. If not, the result is stress, and potential change in living quarters, jobs or repeating expensive courses.

I recall teaching some students about their future after they graduated. Many, at 18 years of age, thought that moving away from home while they were going to university would be a great plan. When we did a sample budget of how much that decision would cost them, compared to staying home while attending school, they were shocked. Without a doubt, creating a budget, getting real with the financial facts and planning to save each pay day for essential things like school fees for the next term and warmer clothes for the seasons were more important than parties, eating out, and buying clothes they didn't need.

Your Job Earnings Equal Your Take Home Pay

If you work for a minimum wage, learn what that is in your new location, as the wages vary in each province in Canada and each American state. Determine if you have savings you can rely on or if your family can assist you financially, if necessary. Remember that with earned income, there are taxes and other deductions from your income, so your take-home pay (net income) that you deposit in the bank is lower than you may expect.

The deductions that will be taken from a person's pay depend on several factors, including their tax status, income level and the province or territory in which they work. Some standard deductions typically taken from Canadian paychecks include federal and provincial income taxes, Canada Pension Plan (CPP) and Employment Insurance (EI) premiums.

Example:

The total income for someone earning $16.75 an hour for 20 hours a week in Canada would be $335.00 per week. When you receive your paycheque, you will note several deductions from your pay, and the amount you receive is less than what you may have expected. Based on 24 pay periods (paid twice a month on the 15th and 30th)), your gross pay for 40 hours of work each month will be **$670.00**, and after the deductions, your net earnings (or take-home pay) will be approximately **$602.25.** By adding the federal and provincial income taxes, CPP contributions, and EI premiums, your deductions will be **$67.74**.

Although payroll is based on each individual as well as the company they work for, here is a basic example for your paycheque:

Pay period frequency: twice a month (15th and 30th of each month)

Total tax deductions on income	$25.63
CPP deductions	$31.19
EI deductions	$10.92
Total deductions	**$67.74**
Net amount for each paycheque	$602.26
Net Monthly Amount	$1,204.52

Created by the Payroll Deductions Online Calculator

Realistically, you can only create a budget with your net income or the money you receive. You can find a budget template on my website. Once you know your income, calculate your real expenses. Did you know, for example, that when you sign a lease for rental accommodation, you can be expected to pay for one and a half months' rent before you move in? The landlord can use the half month's rent as a security deposit for damages or failure to pay before you leave. Read the lease carefully and ask questions if it is not clear.

Example:

Your new place will cost you $1200 per month.

However, before you move in, you'll have to pay the landlord $1800 ($1200 + $600). If you have taken good care of your lodgings, and there are no damages, you will be refunded the half month's deposit.

Other Expenses

You can expect other expenses such as the Internet, cable TV, electricity, heat, parking, etc. Some rental costs may include these, but most won't. And these expenses are pretty much necessities. This will not include transportation, food, clothing, furniture, or other items to set up your home. My website lists places to purchase gently used items to set up your home, and there are some suggestions later in this book. (www.joannemarlow.com/employmentguide)

Other items that seem to cost more than expected include entertainment, food, transportation, and activities. While at university or work, spending money on added snacks, coffees, smoothies, and meals adds up to more than you may expect. You will be amazed at how much money you will save if you bring your drinks, snacks and meals to school or work. In addition, your homemade food will likely be healthier. I know…I sound like your mother!

WHAT'S NEXT? · 43

Meal Type	Breakfast	Lunch	Dinner	Snack	Daily	Five days
Light	Original Blend Coffee $1.92 Blueberry Donut $1.74	Soup $4.29 Steeped Tea $1.92	Chili 5.49 Iced Coffee $2.33	Old Fashion Plain Donut	$19.20	$96.00
Totals	$3.66	$6.21	$7.82	$1.51		
Medium	Farmer's Breakfast Sandwich $5.25 Orange Juice $2.68	Ham & Cheddar Sandwich $5.99 Freshly Brewed Iced Tea Quencher $2.21 Chocolate Chunk Cookie $1.51	Cilantro Lime Veggie Wrap $6.79 Peach Real Fruit Quencher $2.68 Chocolate Chip Muffin $2.09	Potato wedges	$31.69	$158.45
Totals	$7.93	$9.71	$11.56	$2.49		
Full	Bagel B.E.L.T. $5.99 Vanilla Cream Cold Brew $3.26 Fruit Explosion Muffin $2.56	Turkey Bacon Club Sandwich $6.79 Hershey S'mores Iced Capp $4.08 Peanut Butter Cookies $1.51	Chipotle Steak Bowl $9.99 Gold Peak Raspberry $3.50 Boston Cream donut $1.74	Donut bites 20 pack	$43.41	$217.05
Totals	$11.81	$12.38	$15.23	$3.99		

Example:

Based on a popular fast-food restaurant, the amounts above are a sample of costs based on daily expenditures for five days a week when you may be on campus or working. (June 2023).

Treat yourself once a week rather than five to seven days a week. It doesn't take long to spend more money than you expected when you could just as easily spend a few minutes planning your meals and snacks, make them the night before and take them to school or work. In 14 weeks (e.g., a semester), you can **save between $1,344 - $3038**.

Chapter Five

SETTING THE STAGE FOR EMPLOYMENT

What are the Differences Between a Curriculum Vitae and a Résumé?

In North America, a Curriculum Vitae (CV) is used primarily by high-ranking managers and professionals, including professors, government or federal positions, and academic researchers. The CV documents your life-long work history, academic accomplishments, and any publications with your name. Besides work history and education, it includes awards, publications, and professional affiliations. It has no page limit. Most CVs tend to be two-to-three pages long, but if you have a lot of experience behind you, they can exceed ten pages.

The majority of positions will require a résumé. Compared to a CV, résumés present a "summary" of your work history, education, skills, awards, certifications, licenses and interests. It is typically one page and may extend to two if you have multiple work experiences.

> *Recruiters will spend only 6 - 10 seconds to read your résumé.*

Résumé Overview

A résumé is the best way to sell yourself. It is a formal typed document that describes specific information so that the employer can determine if you have the right experience, skills, and attitudes they seek. Most people don't prepare a "great" résumé, and I will give you a head start on being awesome and ahead of other candidates.

First, you need to know that employers get hundreds, sometimes thousands, of résumés each week. The shock is that most recruiters spend an average of **six to ten seconds** reviewing each résumé. They seek specific information outlining the keywords that describe your skills that indicate you are the person they want! They will either skim-read each résumé or, in many businesses, the résumé is scanned with special software searching for keywords. Either way, the process is quick, and the person in charge of reviewing the résumés sorts them into three piles: Keep, Maybe and Discard.

1. **Keep** - Recruiters read most of the résumé and consider you for an initial interview.

2. **Maybe** - After they've read the résumés to keep, this pile "may" receive a more detailed look.

3. **Discard** - These résumés go directly into the garbage or are deleted.

Sadly, most employers do NOT respond to your applications unless you are considered for an interview. Continuing your search is the best use of your time. Please do NOT wait for them to call you. Your job is finding a job, so keep taking action to apply to as many jobs as possible.

The format for the résumé in the following pages is designed for adults (ages 18 – 50) who are new to Canada, taking courses or getting a Canadian degree. This guide will also be valuable to working-age people seeking work or promotions. Although you will find many résumé templates online, the one I have developed has been highly regarded and accepted by employers. That's not to say you can't be unique in your style and format for your résumé. Remember that the reader MUST be able to read your most important information in the six to ten seconds allotted. Keep the résumé attractive, clear and informative.

Your Résumé

I have edited and created peoples' résumés for decades. Even though editing someone else's résumé tends to be easy for some people, I know that writing about oneself can be daunting. You don't want to sound boastful, yet you don't want to exclude any essential points. Some of you may not have ever prepared a résumé before or for a long time and haven't a clue where to begin. This is an excellent chapter to help you.

Most employers start reading at the beginning of the first page, then decide whether to read further. I can't emphasize the importance of including your skills summary or profile at the beginning of your résumé, which includes your strengths, employable characteristics and achievements. That's likely all the recruiter will read before selecting a destination "pile" for your résumé.

As mentioned previously, more companies are now using AI scanning software to select the most suitable résumés based on your inclusion of *keywords*. Scanned résumés will be used when specific keywords describe the qualities or experiences essential to the company. Seek and use the keywords used in the job description advertisement. Some examples for some jobs might be: managing, organizing, planning, electrical, or technology. Even though your skills may be excellent, you may be bypassed if your résumé is incorrectly worded. After the initial scan, it's up to the recruiter to continue assessing or taking action to contact you for an interview.

Do You Need More Than One Résumé?

Typically, you can use the same résumé for many different job applications. However, suppose you are applying to more than one field or industry (e.g., retail service versus web design *or* manufacturing versus business administration). It would be best to tailor your résumé to each industry, listing your relevant strengths. However, the only part you will need to change is your Skills Summary, where you will emphasize the applicable skills that are either transferable or specific to the advertised job. To fit your credentials for different industries, I suggest you add those particular skills to your cover letter rather than your résumé.

What About Format?

The format of a résumé is essential. Within one to two pages, it has to have key points, white space balance (space that has no words), and essential information about you and what you have to offer. This is not necessarily a time to look "really" different from others unless you apply for a highly creative job and want to showcase your creativity. Generally, you will want a neat, professional-looking résumé that correctly outlines your skills and is easy for the recruiter to read your important credentials.

The Résumé is Your Advertisement

Think of the résumé as an advertisement for yourself. The employer wants to know what you can do, what you've done, and what you're involved in during your spare time. It is the well-rounded person who will be considered first. Like advertisements, you must outline the "benefits" of hiring you. Even if you have had minimal experience or you've been in one job all your life, your involvement in your community, school, and life will also speak volumes. Your work and volunteer experience must describe your experience, accomplishments, and responsibilities. This is not the time to be modest. You can brag a bit about your accomplishments, but be factual and **never exaggerate or lie!** During the interview, you'll be asked to substantiate and give examples of your facts and experiences. Often, your references will be asked about the quality of your work listed from various experiences on your résumé. Just remember that you are already amazing and will learn how to "sell" your skills and strengths properly through the information in this book.

Should You Hire a Professional to Write Your Résumé?

If you don't have the confidence to prepare your résumé, you can hire a professional résumé writer to create a résumé. In this case, you'll go through an in-depth interview, and the writer will design your résumé and charge you a fee. It will be extra if you want it printed or put on a USB stick. Hiring someone to prepare your résumé can cost upwards of $500 or more (over $2000 for an executive position), depending on your background and the work you seek.

Be Prepared at All Times

There's nothing worse than seeing an ad for a job you'd love to apply for, and your résumé isn't finished or updated. I recommend updating your résumé at least every year and after every job or promotion so that you are ready for those "just in time" and often perfect job opportunities. There's nothing worse than seeing the deadline come and go and you don't have a current copy of your résumé prepared. I learned that from personal experience.

Writing your Résumé

Some people will prepare their résumés and will search online to select a template from the Internet. Others will upload their résumé through a scanning ATS App with their own format, using multiple tables and a fee for each document it prepares. ATS stands for *application tracking system*. This is a computer software program that saves employers time and money. It does this by automating job applicants' tracking, assessment, and selection. My only caution is that most people rely on these Apps, and I suggest that if you want to "stand out," you will craft something that will actually get read by a scanning App software **and** a human. I designed a format that continually gets rave reviews from employers, allowing the reader to review your most prominent attributes and accomplishments within the six to ten seconds they give you.

In the following pages, I've explained the essential parts of a résumé. There is no guarantee that your résumé will be read in its entirety or even where the reader will begin; however, if it is well structured and highlighted, the reader can pick and choose the parts of your résumé that interest them.

Proof-Read to Achieve Zero Errors

Before sending a résumé anywhere, please ensure that someone else has proofread it. They should look for errors in grammar, punctuation, sentence structure, format, vocabulary and spelling errors and help you correct them. Having another set of eyes review your résumé will help you present yourself clearly and professionally.

A résumé should be reviewed at least three to five times before sending it to an employer. I can attest to the embarrassment you may feel when a potential employer finds an error in your résumé during the interview!

A polished résumé will open the doors to more job opportunities in less time and potentially higher earnings, assuming you have good skills and will learn to use the résumé effectively in your job search.

What if You Lack Experience?

I remember a client who was being trained as an administrative assistant who no prior work experience. She was a stay-at-home mom and wanted to enter the workplace as soon as her children entered high school. Her previous experience involved organizing "hot dog days" for the elementary school. Believe it or not, I was able to provide her with an impressive one-and-half-page résumé that listed her employable transferrable skills and her new office skills. She landed an administrative job with a large insurance company. There are no excuses for not having an excellent résumé. If you know yourself and what attitudes, skills and strengths you can bring to an employer, you can write an impressive résumé. This is also an excellent opportunity to think about what "transferable skills" you already have. Many employers welcome someone they can train who demonstrates a great work attitude and ethics.

Think also of any time you have volunteered to help in an organization. These might include your place of worship, a sports team, a club, a senior's home or assisted living, soup kitchens, babysitting, tutoring, dog walking, looking after plants and animals while your neighbours are on vacation, shovelling snow or washing cars for fundraising. Any school clubs or organizations, work experiences, job shadows, or internships that you took part in or held a role of responsibility would also be important.

Your career center, a career coach or a professional can help you with your résumé. As a result, you'll receive an education in self-awareness, personal branding and career knowledge that you can leverage through the years.

Automation Used by Recruiters

Some organizations use unique APPs to track the keywords of all applications. The Applicant Tracking Systems (ATS) speeds up the process of reviewing hundreds of applications without a "human" spending time reading each résumé and cover letter. As mentioned, Applicant Tracking Systems (ATS) are software applications used by recruiters and hiring managers to manage the entire recruitment process, from posting job openings to selecting interview candidates. The primary function of an ATS is to automate the recruitment process by collecting and storing résumés and other applicant information in a centralized database. In addition to streamlining the recruitment process, ATS also ensures compliance with legal requirements and helps to eliminate bias in the screening process.

Many ATS providers are available in Canada, including international and domestic vendors. Popular ATS systems used by Canadian recruiting companies include Taleo, iCIMS, SmartRecruiters, Jobvite, and Workday. For a student to use one of these Apps to create a résumé, cover letter, or other services, there is a nominal fee for single and multiple uses.

I tested one of the ATS Apps and was somewhat disappointed with how they reconfigured a résumé. Maybe I'm biased, but I found the format of their suggested résumés to be complicated, with multiple tables and cells (which added to my frustration when I had to make changes). Also, they added a profile paragraph, which in my opinion, will only be read by a machine, and not a human.

When candidates submit their résumé and application, the ATS automatically scans the document and analyses relevant information such as their work history, education, and skills. The system then assigns a score to the application based on how closely it matches the job requirements.

Recruiters can use the ATS to search and filter the candidate pool based on specific criteria such as years of experience, education level, and specific skills. The system also allows recruiters to track the progress of each candidate through the hiring process, schedule interviews, and communicate with candidates.

In addition to these core functions, some ATS systems may include additional features such as job board integration, candidate relationship management (CRM), and analytics reporting.

Overall, an ATS streamlines the recruitment process, saves time, and helps recruiters find the best-fit candidates for the job. However, be aware that some recruiters must balance using an ATS with a human touch to ensure that the best candidates are not overlooked due to a rigid application review process. That's why a follow-up call or email is often a good step to bring your "name" to the top of the list. You can ask if your application was received.

Small business owners may not use ATS Apps and will read (quickly scan) the applications.

Parts of a Résumé

Personal Information

Sometimes I have seen résumés needing more contact information at the top of the page. This is essential to a résumé so that you can be quickly contacted. It should include the following:

Your full name (also add your "English" or nickname, if applicable), complete mailing address (or at least your city), province/territory/state, postal code, personal email address and telephone number where you can be reached. Employers will want to know if you must travel a long distance from home to your workplace. Some worksites lack transit, and walking or travelling long distances may prevent you from being considered, especially if snowfall or inclement weather affects transportation and restricts you from being on time for work.

Skills Summary

Since the reader will only scan your résumé briefly, the Skills Summary gives a snapshot of who you are. This summary highlights your characteristics, achievements, and strengths and allows the reader to identify your best qualities, skills, personality and accomplishments. It should coincide with the requirements listed in the advertisement. Your information is often taken from the details of your work experience but lists only your best and applicable skills. I am passionate about making sure you enjoy using all those skills. If you think about it, we all excel at something. You likely received better grades in certain subjects or in learning through various methods, such as reading, taking action, or creating something. That is the same with a job where you want to feel useful, challenged, and productive. I recall a person who had an interview for a very senior role. Although he could do financial budgets and forecasting, he knew that he would be unhappy by crunching numbers for any more than 40% of his tasks. He preferred to be a problem solver, using his critical thinking skills. It will enable the *Work Experience* section to be briefer while taking your best talents from all jobs and putting them into the Skills Summary category. As a small warning, this section of your résumé takes time and will likely be the more difficult part of creating your résumé. You can replace Skills Summary with any of the following headings: Skills Summary, Profile, or Professional Profile.

Below are some suggestions to consider for the Skills Summary section.

- **A Bulleted List –** The Skills Summary contains a six to eight-bulleted list of your best personal and professional information that will offer the WOW factor to your résumé. The summary can be altered or prioritized to suit the main focus of each field of jobs you apply for (e.g., sports, sales, research, fine arts, retail, hospitality, conservation, education, construction, education, management, health, and film). Typically, the order of your skills should apply to the industry/job. (e.g., skills for a construction job should list your carpentry skills before organization skills).

- **Use Key Words for Credibility** – Ensure you use the keywords from the advertisement or job description regarding your qualifications, experience, and attributes. These scanners will search for your credentials, sort the resumes and then employers will review the final selected resumes to determine whom they will interview.

- **Compatibility** – Today, companies seek people who are engaged in their work and share the company's values. Look up the company's website to learn more about the company and its values. Add a line to your Skills Summary stating actions, behaviours, or important causes that you value (e.g., the environment, giving to the community or charity, transparent communication and collaboration, recognition, and accountability). Recruiters also seek employees who share and align with their organization's values, goals and expected behaviours.

- **Identify Your Strengths** – In addition to the advertisement, use resources such as your personality assessments (e.g., Myers Briggs, StrengthsFinder 2.0), language from reference letters that describe you, and words from other pleasing advertisements that apply to you. For example, from the Myers Briggs ENFJ descriptor, I have italicized the words below that would be ideal to consider in your résumé Skills Summary.

ENFJs are natural-born *charismatic leaders* full of *passion*. Forming around two percent of the population, they are often our politicians, coaches and teachers, reaching out and *inspiring others to achieve* and *do good* in the world. With a *natural confidence that begets influence*, ENFJs take great pride and joy in *guiding others* to *work together* to *improve themselves and their community*.

Make sure you use the descriptors from your Personality test results. If you haven't taken the Myers-Briggs Preference Survey, here is a free link: **www.16personalities.com**. By placing the four letters (e.g., ENFJ) into your search engine and selecting the Careers tab, you can get a basic idea of the careers that might be best for you. They will also describe your personality strengths which may come in handy for adding to your cover letter or résumé.

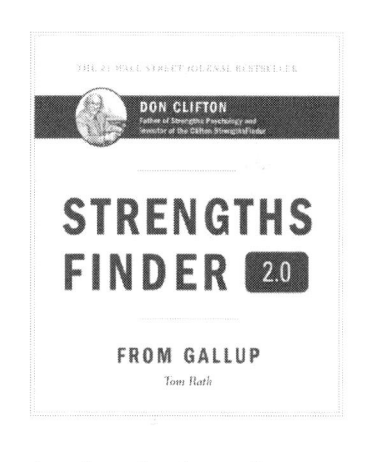

I also recommend doing the assessment from **StrengthsFinder 2.0™** by Tom Rath (mentioned earlier). This is an excellent way to determine the best vocabulary describing your top strengths to a potential employer and learn how to overcome your weaknesses. This book also has a new version, "**Now, Discover Your Strengths**" by Donald Clifton and Marcus Buckingham. You can find several sample tests on the Internet, but by far, the best, in my opinion, still comes from this book. An assessment code comes with both books, and you can do the assessment online and within a brief time, the results are emailed to you. The book will then provide more details, scenarios, and ways to use your strengths in the workplace. I have used both books; the newer version is more reasonably priced. Undoubtedly, the incredible phrases written to describe your personal and innate strengths will make your confidence soar. On page 37, I explained how using this assessment for my personal applications and cover letters made a shocking difference in getting interviews.

- **Create a List** – For your employability skills, strengths, and characteristics, write your experiences or personal examples that verify these qualities. This list and your examples will prepare you for an excellent interview, as you will be asked to give examples of how you used some of your strengths.

- **Special Skills** – If you are fluent in speaking and writing multiple languages, including English, enter this information into the Skills Summary. Add any software and technology skills in this category, as well. If your desired industry requires you to use specific software, mention that you know it.

- **Common Attributes and Accomplishments** – Group your accomplishments together (community service, awards, long-term involvement, contributions to society) and list the most important ones that apply or are relevant to the industry or job.

- **Relevance to the Job** – Ensure you put the most meaningful information at the top of the list. Only include information that is <u>relevant</u> to the jobs you are considering.

- **Use Action Words** – Use clear language that brings your work experience to life. Use action words rather than passive words and non-action verbs. Strong action verbs, as listed on the following pages, used with explicit language to outline exemplary achievements are essential parts of a well-constructed résumé. Phrases like "provided" and "organized" are overused, monotonous, and add no value to your résumé.

Instead of using passive language, which describes *doing*:

e.g., *Negotiated contracts with vendors*

I suggest action language, which describes *achieving the following*:

e.g., *Slashed administration costs by 25% by pricing negotiation options.*

A change like this makes a dramatic improvement. On the following page, you'll find a great selection of helpful action words and phrases to begin describing your skills and characteristics. Get your highlighter pen out and search for your action descriptors. Once you have highlighted some skills, list your tasks or responsibilities where these action words were used. Doing this exercise also prepares you for your interview, as it will offer credibility to your experience.

Action Words and Phrases for Résumé Development

The following phrases and words may help with organizing your résumé statements. They concisely convey accomplishments, making your résumé more readable.

ACTION WORDS		SKILLS	PERSONAL QUALITIES	
Accomplished	Gathered	Accounting	Accountable	Humorous
Achieved	Generated	Artistic	Adaptable	Imaginative
Administered	Guided	Communication	Aggressive	Incisive
Arranged	Helped	Computational	Amiable	Independent
Assisted	Implemented	Computer	Ambitious	Innovative
Acquired	Improved	Creative-thinking	Approachable	Integrity
Acted/Functioned	Initiated	Critical thinking	Broad-minded	Intuitive
Balanced	Instructed	Customer service	Business-like	Leader
Bargained	Interpreted	Decision-making	Calm	Likeable
Budgeted	Investigated	Editing	Cheerful	Loyal
Built	Learned	Entrepreneurial	Common-sense	Mature
Chaired	Led	Fundraising	Compatible	Meticulous
Coached	Maintained	Development	Competent	Motivated
Communicated	Managed	Interpersonal	Confident	Objective
Compiled	Motivated	Keyboarding	Congenial	Optimistic
Completed	Negotiated	Leadership	Conscientious	Patient
Composed	Operated	Listening	Considerate	Perceptive
Conducted	Organized	Management	Consistent	Persuasive
Considered	Originated	Math	Cooperative	Personable
Constructed	Participated	Mediation	Courteous	Pleasant
Controlled	Preformed	Organizational	Creative	Positive
Coordinated	Planned	People	Customer-	Practical
Counselled	Prepared	presentation	oriented	Professional
Created	Presented	Problem-solving	Dedicated	Progressive
Decided	Produced	Reading	Dependable	Punctual
Decreased	Programmed	reasoning	Diligent	Quick-learner
Delegated	Promoted	Research	Diplomatic	Reliable
Delivered	Recorded	Speaking	Diversity	Resourceful
Demonstrate	Repaired	Supervisory	Down-to-earth	Respected
Designed	Researched	Teamwork	Dynamic	Responsible
Developed	Scheduled	Technical	Eager	Self-reliant
Directed	Served	Thinking	Efficient	Sensible
Edited	Set-up	Verbal	Energetic	Sensitive
Educated	Sketched	Writing	Enterprising	Sincere
Employed	Sold		Enthusiastic	Steady
Encouraged	Specialized		Fair	Supportive
Established	Supervised		Flexible	Tactful
Evaluated	Taught		Friendly	Team player
Executed	Terminated		Genuine	Thorough
Experienced	Trained		Goal-oriented	Thoughtful
Explained	Trouble-shot		Gracious	Trustworthy
Focused	Upgraded		Hard-working	Well-liked
Fabricated	Verified		Healthy	Willing
Facilitated	Worked		Honesty	
Fundraised	Wrote			

Education and Training

This relevant section may be the deciding factor, especially for higher positions. It should include all your formal education, degrees, certificates, and diplomas – anything related to proper training.

- ◆ **Where to begin** – Keep the entire list in reverse chronological order, starting with the most recent education or training. If you are new to this country, list your current educational institution, location, area of study, and expected graduation date/year.

- ◆ **Institutions** – List the names and locations of the schools attended (If you already have university or college degrees, avoid listing secondary school education). Remember to add the location (city, state/province and country) when you list your education. This is especially important when you list institutions outside your new country. Don't make the reader guess where you had previous training.

- ◆ **Certifications** – Insert the names of certificates, diplomas and proficiency certificates, including their earned dates.

- ◆ **Additional courses** – Certificates or courses, seminars earned for professional development, First Aid training, Food Safe, sales, Microsoft Office, etc. The courses should apply to the position you are seeking. Adding "horseback riding certification" when applying for an administrative job is irrelevant.

Work and Volunteer Experience

- **Keep it Brief** – The descriptions for this section are usually brief, as your most important skills are in your Skills Summary. This also invites interesting and probing questions from the interviewer about your work. You don't want to tell them everything you were responsible for; instead, give them the highest accomplishment or position.

- **List Your Responsibilities** – Depending on your age, you may have a long list of employers, while others may have only one or two. The important thing is to give the employer some idea of how your responsibilities and knowledge increased over the years.

- **Career or Job Gaps** – Almost everyone will have gaps in their work experience for several reasons. Employers need to understand why there is a substantial break in your employment. Since it is always a vital question for an employer, I often recommend adding a reason if there is more than a six-month gap between jobs. (e.g., maternity or paternity leave, raising children, travelling for two years, a personal illness, or looking after ailing parents). Try to think about what the reader will question and then provide an answer before they can ask you the question.

    > *You can interchange **Education** with **Work Experience**, depending on which has more content.*

- **Other Work Activities** – Make sure you include the following in your employment list, even if you weren't paid:

job shadows, co-op work experience, internships, full-time employment, volunteer work, and part-time or shared employment.

Any jobs not relevant to your application or where you worked for a very brief time (a couple of weeks or months - unless it was contracted or temporary work) can be eliminated, especially if they don't leave you with substantial working gaps.

- **Format** – List all your jobs in reverse chronological order, starting with your most recent job, your job title, and the month and year you were employed. If you have had any experience in your new country, list it, regardless of the job. Employers are seeking workers who have had some experience in this country. Never state that you quit or were fired from a job. Include the organization's name and location (city, province/state/country). Add a brief description of the duties that you performed. Be concise, as your Skills Summary will have the transferrable and technical skills from your jobs. e.g., *Responsible for opening and closing the restaurant, serving customers and ensuring all service staff were well trained*

Use a font design that is easy to read: New Times Roman, Arial, Calibri, Cambria, or Helvetica, for example, and depending on the length of your résumé, you can use a font size of 12, 11, or 10.5. Most résumés are online, and the reader can expand the résumé for easier reading.

Interests and Community Involvement

This section demonstrates that you have a life other than work and education. It lends to your credibility and sense of life/work balance. You never know…perhaps the company will want you on their soccer team! Include a short list of interests, achievements, recreational activities, and community involvement if there is room on your résumé.

- **Descriptions** – Indicate the amount of community involvement and the time devoted to the activity (e.g., three years as the soccer assistant coach).

- **Accomplishments** – Indicate any personal or team-based achievements (e.g., Organized the Terry Fox Run in my community for two years; was editor of my university's newsletters).

- **Positions of responsibility** – Indicate positions of responsibility you held. (e.g., Member of the Business Club or Treasurer for the Graduation Committee).

References

References are no longer required on a résumé. However, when you go for an interview, you should have a typed list of at least three references from qualified managers or supervisors from previous jobs to give to the employer or interviewer. You can also email the list to the employer immediately after the interview.

Your references must include people who can attest to and speak highly about your qualifications, character, personality, work ethic and skills. I recall a previous employee who asked me to be a reference, and within seconds, I received an email requesting my reference from the company she applied to. Not only was I unprepared, but I also had attended a Human Rights Tribunal court case against this woman several years before. I answered the employer's questions truthfully, and consequently, the woman did not get the job. The result would likely have been the same if I had declined the candidate's request. Asking permission from people who can support you well before you use their name is critical to your interview, as reputable employers will most likely check all your references.

On the reference page, indicate the person's name, position, company address, telephone number, and email address. Most references are contacted by email, so location is no longer important. Also, *letters of reference* are not particularly read due to a lack of validation. Referees will be asked to comment on your attendance and promptness, quality of work, strengths, anything that would keep you from doing a complete and quality job, and whether they would hire you again.

- **Get permission** – ALWAYS ask your referees for their permission before you list them on a reference sheet. Depending on the positions you are applying to, familiarize your referee with your skills and the jobs you want. Send them your résumé so they can see how you have progressed, and let them know about the types of jobs you seek.

- **Ensure they have seen your work** – Choose people who have supervised you or been in a managing position. Potential employers are more interested in your work references and won't consider personal references. If you are in a position where you can't supply a recent employer (because you are still working for them, or they may not give you a good reference), then a co-worker in a higher position than yourself, a project manager, or someone from previous employment would suffice. Please don't offer names from friends, and do not use relatives. Although your mother will usually praise you, she is not an appropriate referee for a job!

- **List recent references** – Choosing someone you worked with five years ago may not be in your best interest, especially if you have completed additional skills or education. They will not be able to speak to your current situation but will give only the information based on their experience with you. I recall a reference I talked to regarding a young woman I was considering for an accounting position. Her contact was unaware that she had completed a six-year accounting degree and told me she was not more than a bookkeeper. Be careful whom you use as a reference! Or update them on your education, résumé and progress.

- **Alternate references** – If you lack employment and references, using a contact from your school (a favourite instructor, counsellor), sports, volunteer work, a neighbour you have helped, or even your religious leader can be appropriate. Think of a person who is pleased with your behaviour, punctuality, personality, skills, traits/characteristics and can attest to an experience they have observed or heard regarding your success.

Résumé Tips to Remember

Many of you may not have updated your résumé in years, so note that many rules have changed. And now that you are in a new country, the following rules apply. Later, you'll see the application of these rules in résumé examples.

- **Avoid some information** – Do not include your age, sex, race, marital status, health condition, and Social Insurance Number. Do not refer to any specific political or religious affiliations. This information is not required on a résumé.

- **Be consistent** – Leave equal line spacing between each section and subheadings.

- **Use one font only** – However, CAPITALS, **bolding** and *italics*, or a change in font size may add emphasis. Again, keep it consistent, neat and tidy. Some candidates use a pleasing colour for their main headings (e.g., dark blue, forest green, dark grey). For a professional look, avoid bright colours, and do not use colour in your content… keep it to main headings.

- **Abbreviations** – Do NOT use abbreviations (e.g., Feb., &, Ave., St. N. Van. or the word "etc."). Countries, provinces or states can be abbreviated (BC, ON, PQ, MX, CA, FL, WA).

- **Objective** – If you want to add an OBJECTIVE or VISION at the top of your résumé, it should speak to the employer about the value you can bring to their business. Many people make the mistake of asking what the company can offer them.

(e.g., "Seeking a company that will increase my professional development and team building skills and utilize my organizational skills.") Instead, you can write, "A position of responsibility where my management and problem-solving skills will be used to build team production and effectiveness." Note that this information is typically unnecessary when you supply a cover letter.

- **Headings** – If possible, keep all the information under a significant heading on the same page. If you must carry the information to another page, state the title again. e.g., **EXPERIENCE** (cont.)

- **Keep it short** – Keep the résumé under two pages. Use white or ivory (off-white) bond paper if you deliver the résumé in person or by post. If you email your résumé, create it as a document (MS Word) and attach only the PDF file version. However, most companies will tell you the format they prefer. Do NOT put a résumé as part of the body of the email message. That would resemble writing a résumé on lined paper with a pencil. Very tacky!

- **Sending the résumé** – Note that many organizations will only accept your application electronically. Follow their instructions explicitly, or you will end up deleted! Only a very small percentage of companies will respond that they have received your application, and most won't respond to you unless you are to be interviewed. That's another reason your cover letter and résumé must be written professionally or at least look like they were done professionally. I believe that not responding to applicants takes the importance of human connection out of the equation, as efficient as it might be for the organization.

- **No errors** – There should be NO spelling or grammatical errors. Have someone with outstanding English editing skills read your work several times. Typically, résumés with errors in punctuation or grammar are tossed out. It may be assumed that you are not detail-oriented.

- **Don't use "I"** – DO NOT write in the first person (e.g., "I did this" and "I was responsible for…"). Instead, write using action words and phrases. See the examples on the next pages.

- **Bullet points** – Remember that phrases using bullet points do not require a period. Complete sentences require a period.

- **Save your résumé** – Save your document with your name and date on a USB drive and in a separate folder on your computer's hard drive (e.g., Chou, J_11.23). Back it up. Before you send it electronically, save it as a PDF file. Always send the PDF file unless the employer asks for a different format.

- **Résumés for other uses** – Tailor your résumé to suit its purpose (e.g., employment, contracts, or post-secondary education applications).

- **Be HONEST** – Your qualifications will be tested during your interview or reference checks. About a third of people embellish their educational qualifications; however, in the end, you could be fired or even charged with fraud.

- **Headings and lists** – Avoid having a major title with only one point. If possible, combine it with another heading. (e.g., Interests: Fishing). Instead, combine "fishing" with other recreational interests, hobbies, or community involvement. (e.g., Outdoor sports such as fishing, mountain biking, camping and hiking).

- **Printed résumés** – For résumés you print, only use one side of each page for your résumé and number the pages in the footer. This is important if the reader accidentally drops your résumé on the floor or gets mixed up with other résumés. Make sure you use a header or footer on subsequent pages to indicate page numbers and ownership.

- **Presentation** – Place the typed résumé in a large envelope and avoid folding or crinkling the résumé. Presentation counts. Don't staple your résumé; use a paper clip. Place your cover letter on top, loose.

- **Keep it simple** – Creativity to get noticed is unnecessary these days, although a hand-delivered résumé may get noticed.

Résumé Information Worksheet

You can complete this worksheet before creating your résumé. This will give you the essential information in draft form so that you have everything on one page handy before you type your résumé, no matter what format you use. It will also serve as a history of your work and accomplishments. You will also find this in the employment guide on my website.

Name
Address
City, Province   Postal Code
Phone #   Email

SKILLS SUMMARY

(What are your specific skills, characteristics, and specialties that you have that will be relevant for this job). List at least 5-8 bullets, with semi-colons separating similar skills or qualifications.

(E.g., • Portrays as a collaborative leader; visionary; situational and highly creative problem-solver

-
-
-
-
-
-
-

EDUCATION AND TRAINING (list All education, training, and certificates)

Institution	
Degree:	Dates
Institution	
Degree:	Dates
Institution:	
Degree:	Dates
Institution:	
Degree:	Dates
Institution:	
Degree:	Dates

EMPLOYMENT AND VOLUNTEER EXPERIENCE

Position/Title	Company Name, Location	Dates Worked
Responsibilities:		

Position/Title	Company Name, Location	Dates Worked
Responsibilities:		

Position/Title	Company Name, Location	Dates Worked
Responsibilities:		

Position/Title	Company Name, Location	Dates Worked
Responsibilities:		

Position/Title	Company Name, Location	Dates Worked
Responsibilities:		

Position/Title	Company Name, Location	Dates Worked
Responsibilities:		

ACCOMPLISHMENTS: (This includes all awards, honours, acknowledgements, etc.) If this doesn't apply to you, then leave this section out.

Achievements	Year Accomplished/Received
•	
•	
•	
•	

INTERESTS AND COMMUNITY INVOLVEMENT: (list the activities and organizations you were involved in

- •   •
- •   •

References

Do not add references to your résumé. Instead, create a <u>Separate Page</u> with your references for the interviewer (or when asked).

Reference name, Position	Phone
Company name and address	Email address
Reference name, Position	Phone
Company name and address	Email address
Reference name, Position	Phone
Company name and address	Email address
Reference name, Position	Phone
Company name and address	Email address

Putting Your Skills on Paper

Now you need to market yourself to employers. Creating a professional-looking résumé with specific descriptions of your skills, strengths, and qualifications will be easier after completing the homework on "yourself." This will include determining your core values and strengths, experiences or responsibilities you genuinely enjoy, and tasks that motivate and excite you.

If you have a career goal, do your best to select entry-level jobs related to your destination. For example, if you wish to be in law, apply to work in a law office and start with jobs involving administrative tasks or assisting the law team. Or, if you are interested in construction project management, work for a construction company and assist in managing projects, or pivot to gain the apprenticeship that will take you to a journeyman position. One of my students wanted to be a graphic designer, and her first entry-level jobs were in a camera shop, followed by a picture framing company. In both jobs, she learned more about cameras, their operation, and helping clients; she also learned how to cut glass and choose the right matt and frames for large and small paintings and prints. Both skills were needed for her education and career in Graphic Design. She now owns a thriving graphic design company.

Next, you'll prepare a cover letter for <u>each</u> job application, practice for the interview, and create follow-up thank you letters after every interview. With so much competition for each job, it is imperative that you are well prepared and know what skills and attributes you can offer the company and what you need from them. Writing about yourself can be challenging, so I have prepared some documents to help you.

In the following chapters, you'll find sample resumes for people who have never had a job to those with years of experience in their own countries. That's what this next chapter is about. So, roll up your sleeves and get ready to take action.

Chapter Six

WRITING THE RÉSUMÉ

Typically, the résumé should showcase your relevant skills, experience, and achievements in a clear and concise format which would be tailored to the job you are applying.

To illustrate what NOT to do, the following résumé was given to me by an entry-level student looking for full-time work in a desired career. Not only was I surprised at the number of errors made in spelling, information, dates, formatting, and information that should never be on a résumé (Social Insurance Number, age, political or spiritual beliefs), the résumé and its contents were useless to the employer since there was no indication of the type of job he wanted or how he could be contacted. First, you will see the "before" and then the same resume after it was "revised."

> Resume of John Smith
>
> Age
> > Seventeen
>
> SIN
> > 123-456-7890
>
> WORK EXPERIENCE
>
> Jan. 2017 - dec. 2018 Busboy,
>
> Jan. -March 2020 Macdonald's fry cook
>
> July & Aug. 2017-18: Apartment block grounds maintenance for friends and family.
>
> Jouly - nov. 2019 : Subway sandwich artist.
>
> VOLUNTEER WORK
>
> Summer 2019 : The Special Olympics Canada games , '10 , Vancouver.
>
> Winter 2018 : Winterfest '18-19 , Vancouver.
>
> Winter 2018-19 : First Night, Vancouver.
>
> HOBBIES AND INTERESTS:
>
> Culinary Studies (Chef's training courses, personal preparation)
>
> Rock Climbing
> > Horseback riding Mechanics

An employer needs to know immediately if a person is suitable for a specific position in their business.

After a brief interview, I reformatted his résumé (See the next page), which my student used. As a result, he had four job offers as a cook apprentice.

Note the differences between the student's version and the revised resume below. It's the same person, but the résumé is written with clearer content and formatted properly.

Revised Version

JOHN SMITH
Apt. #123 - 456 Seventh Street
North Vancouver, BC V7C IV4
Phone: (604) 666-5566

OBJECTIVE To develop my skills as a Cook Apprentice leading to Chef's Red Seal

SKILLS SUMMARY
- Team leader in Cooks Training course at Smith Secondary School
- Excellent interpersonal skills with peers and associates
- Active participant in community organizations
- High energy, dedicated, motivated, dependable worker
- Quick learner, ability to work unsupervised; excellent work ethics
- Honour roll graduate

WORK EXPERIENCE

Fry Cook	McDonald's Restaurant West Vancouver, BC	January 2022 - Present
Food Preparation	Subway North Vancouver, BC	July 2021 - November 2021
Busser, Customer Service	McDonald's Restaurant (Part-time) North Vancouver, BC	January 2020 - July 2021
Grounds Maintenance	Wishing Well Apartments Vancouver and Surrey, BC	Summer, 2020

VOLUNTEER WORK

Display Set up	Aurora Winterfest, Vancouver, BC	Winters, 2021 - 2022
Preparation/Operations	Special Olympics Canada Games, Vancouver, BC	Summer, 2021
Public Assistance	Family First Night Festival (New Year's Eve) Mount Seymour, North Vancouver, BC	Winters, 2018 - 2019

EDUCATION and TRAINING CERTIFICATES

Smith Secondary School, North Vancouver, BC   Graduated June 202_
St. John's Ambulance, Safety Oriented First Aid
Food Safe Certification; Super Host Certification

ACHIEVEMENTS and INTERESTS

Service Award in the Chef's Training Program, Smith Secondary
Honor Roll in Grades 11 and 12
Cooking, rock climbing, horseback riding

Entry-Level Positions Résumé Samples

Suitable for students with little or no previous experience

SERINDA SAWANI

4368 Brentwood Place
North Vancouver, BC V71 4S3
e. ssawani@hotmail.com   m. 778 - 404 -1333

SKILLS SUMMARY

- Excellent interpersonal skills, confident, considerate
- Service-oriented, positive attitude
- Co-operative team member; takes initiative
- Responsible, well organized, completes tasks
- Hard-working, quick learner, and willing to develop new skills
- Active participant in community organizations

EDUCATION

North Shore Secondary School, North Vancouver, BC. Intended Graduation: June 202_
First Aid Babysitting Certificate — September 20__

EXPERIENCE

Earl's Restaurant, West Vancouver, BC
Hostess — August 202_ - March 202_

Canadian Kidney Foundation Fundraising — Winter 2022
Volunteer Canvasser

Babysitting — 2018 – Ongoing
Childcare for children under six years of age

INTERESTS

- Dancing (hip hop and jazz), acting in drama productions
- Babysitting
- Skiing for the school race team
- Basketball, horseback riding

JACQUES PERRAIS
4181 Golf Drive
Quesnel, BC V2J 2K7
Phone: (250) 955-4446
E-mail: jperrais@hotmail.com

SKILLS SUMMARY

- Demonstrates excellent interpersonal skills with clients and colleagues
- Ability to learn new concepts quickly and apply them to my tasks
- Highly motivated, positive attitude; hard-working, focused
- Detailed and well organized; dependable
- Apply excellent computer skills in all my work
- Fluent in English, Mandarin and French

EDUCATION and TRAINING

- Correlieu Secondary School, Quesnel, BC
- Intended Graduation, 202_

WORK and VOLUNTEER EXPERIENCE

Cook	**Panago Pizza** (Part-Time) Preparing pizzas, cleaning, and helping customers	May 2020 – Present
Volunteer	**Salvation Army** Collected clothing for the homeless	January 2018
Job Shadows	**Boston Pizza Restaurant**, Cook Observed a cook's typical day and took part in food preparation	November 2017
	Financial Analyst Experienced the typical day of a financial analyst	November 2016
Volunteer	**Superpages**, Info Book Distribution Delivered over 300 phone books to areas throughout Quesnel	April 2015

EXTRA-CURRICULAR INTERESTS

- Cooking/baking
- Boxing, cross-country running, soccer
- Playing the drums, music

DON MATHEWS
1234 McNellie Drive • Abbotsford, BC V2J 1V4
Phone: (778) 929-1234
Email Address: dmathews@hotmail.com

SUMMARY

- Demonstrates a high level of manual dexterity and repairing things mechanically
- Maintains excellent driving records with BC Driver's License (N)
- Compatible team player, independent and entrepreneurial worker
- Ability to learn new concepts and tasks quickly; skilled problem-solver
- Highly motivated, detail-oriented, and well organized
- Accomplished interpersonal skills, enjoy servicing people
- Practical computer literacy with PC and MacOS systems and the Internet

EDUCATION AND TRAINING

Abby Secondary School, Abbotsford, BC
Expected Graduation: June 202_

CPR Certificate (St. John's Ambulance) March 202_

EXPERIENCE

Chilliwack Honda 20_ - present
Lot Boy

Pacific National Exhibition, Vancouver Summer 20_
Concession Vendor

Champion Sports, BC Place Stadium August 20_
Retail Sales Part Time

H.Y. Louie ~ Crippled Children of BC August 20_
Kiosk Vendor

INTERESTS

- Automobile mechanics – restored a 1967 Mustang, changed the stereo in a car, adjusted signal and headlights, and made oil changes
- Sports - basketball, volleyball, hockey rollerblading, snowboarding, and kayaking
- Electronics - built and fine-tuned a remote-control car
- Music – listening and mixing

This is an acceptable format for references, which can be given to the interviewer if required.

DON MATHEWS
1234 McNellie Drive   Abbotsford, BC   V2J 5X9
m. (778) 992-1234   e. dmathews@hotmail.com

REFERENCES

Mrs. J. Wilson Career and Personal Planning Department Coordinator Prince Secondary School 1234 Learning Road Quesnel, BC V2J 2A6	Phone: 250-992-6789 Ext. 301 Wilsonj@princegeorgesd99.bc.ca
Mr. John Milnor Service Manager Chilliwack Honda 1234 Auto Mall Way Chilliwack, BC V2J 3F5	Phone: 604-991-4321 Jmilnor@fraservalleyhonda.com
Mr. Bill Smith Instructor Technology Department Prince Secondary Community School 4353 Success Avenue Prince George, BC V2J 5X3	Phone: 250-992-6839 Ext. 103 Smithb@PrinceGeorgesd99.bc.ca

College Graduates and Certificate Programs Résumé Samples

Suitable for people who have had some work experience in North America

KIM MACDONALD
4545 Third Street, Port Alberni, BC V9N 1G1
Cell: 250.666.4444   e. kmacdonald@yahoo.com

SKILLS SUMMARY

- Extensive experience in customer service, office administration, and bookkeeping
- Excellent and efficient computer skills - Microsoft Office Suite (Word, Excel, Outlook, PowerPoint), Adobe, QuickBooks, Internet/ social media. Typing speed is over 80 WPM.
- Fluent in English, French, and Spanish with proficient spelling and grammar
- Over-delivers customer service and friendly interpersonal skills to all colleagues and clients
- Proficient in property management administration, budgeting
- Well-organized, efficient problem solver, and calm in a hectic environment

WORK EXPERIENCE

Property Manager   **L & X Management Ltd.**, Vancouver, BC   2017 - Present

- Sole responsibility for managing long-term and short-term accommodation rentals for properties in Vancouver Island and Maui, Hawaii. This position includes hiring and managing staff, handling employee benefits, bookkeeping, budgeting, scheduling tenants and guests, and efficient problem-solving.

Office Manager   **West Vancouver Irrigation**, West Vancouver, BC   2013 – 2016

- Implemented a system to recover thousands of dollars in lost customer debt/back payments. Provided outstanding customer service to over 2,000 customers, including schedules and bookings, invoicing and cash management, payroll, computer skills and learning new software.

CASUAL AND CONTRACT EXPERIENCE   2007 - 2013

Front Desk   **Blackcomb Lodge**, Whistler, BC
                   Provided friendly customer service to international visitors.

Receptionist/SEO   **Jody's Internet Café**, Whistler, BC
                   Provided customer service/front desk, cash management, and website optimization.

Ski Instructor   **Whistler Blackcomb Ltd.**, Whistler, BC

Windsurf Instructor **Rhonda Smith Windsurfing Center**, Oregon

Receptionist   **Vela Windsurf Resort Center**, Venezuela
                   Personal Concierge for customers, assisting them at checking in/out, equipment rentals and arranging and accompanying them for group dinners

Office Administrator **McMillan Thorne & Company Ltd.**
                   Responsible for all office duties, phones, customer service, bookkeeping

Banquet Server   **Westin Resort, Araxis Restaurant**, Whistler BC

Private Tutor   West Vancouver and Whistler, BC
                   Assisted high school students to succeed in all subjects

EDUCATION

Canadian College of Acupuncture and Oriental Medicine, Bedford, NS   Certification   2015 - 2017
Simon Fraser University, Burnaby, BC   Graduated with BBA - Focus: Marketing   2009
Class Afloat Certification, Vancouver, BC   2006

PERSONAL INTERESTS

- Extensive travelling experience to Europe, Mexico, Central America, Australia, Venezuela, South Pacific, Canada, USA
- Outward Bound – Dog-sledding and winter camping
- Tall Ship crew, student and traveller - Class Afloat (August - December 1996)
- Sailed as crew, student and traveller on a working Tall Ship (S/V Concordia) from San-Diego to Bali for four months
- Outward Bound: 21-day Wilderness Survival Course (August 1995)

COMPETITIVE EXPERIENCE

- Competitive Snowboarder: Half-pipe and Racing - FIS Championships (France), Junior World Championships (Japan), National Championships, Provincial Championships, and regional competitions
- Member of the Canadian Junior Snowboard Team
- BC Provincial Champion for snowboard racing
- Competitive Ski Racer - Junior World Championships, Western Canadian Championships, BC Provincial and Regional competitions.
- Competitive Laser II Sailor – Canadian National Championships

ANDREA SAPPOS

1657 East 46th Avenue, Regina, SK S4N 0A1
asappos@gmail.com   +1 639. 589. 0559

SUMMARY:

- Extraordinary-level awareness of customer service in the hospitality field
- Excellent social skills, self-reliant, and attentive to details
- Energetic, responsible, well-organized and committed to outstanding guest services
- Team player; takes initiative and can work independently
- Ability to work in a high volume and high demand environment
- Easy to adapt to new platforms and willing to learn new skills
- Fluent in English and Tagalog

EDUCATION:

City University of Seattle (Vancouver, BC) Graduated: Spring 2023
Bachelor of Arts in Management

John B. Lacson Foundation Maritime University – Molo Inc., Philippines Graduated: 2016
Bachelor of Science in Cruise Ship Management

WORK EXPERIENCE:

JW Marriott Parq Hotel, Vancouver, BC, Canada Jun 2022 - present
Executive Lounge Server (Part-time)

- Maintained cleanliness and condition of bar, bar unit, tables, and other tools
- Requisitioned all necessary supplies, transporting supplies from storeroom to bar set-up area as required
- Forecasted additional meal requirements and communicated special requests to the kitchen

Rosewood Hotel Georgia, Vancouver, BC, Canada Jun 2022 – Aug 2022
Room Attendant (Part-time)

- Maintained complete knowledge of and comply with all departmental policies, service procedures, and standards
- Ensured that standards were maintained daily at a superior level
- Used mobile housekeeping packs with cleaning supplies, amenities, and linens to the assigned guest room and positioned them securely

IKEA, Coquitlam, BC, Canada Feb 2022 - Jun 2022
Food Co-worker (Part-time)

- Ensured that all areas were always in excellent condition and priced fairly
- Checked expiry dates for all food and beverages; ensured safety at all times

ExtendOps BPO, Iloilo City, Philippines Mar 2020- Dec 2021
Frontline Support Representative

- Answering calls and assisting customers with their requests, providing helpful information, answering questions and responding to complaints via email, chat or call
- Listening to and coaching team members with their calls and customer service

Hinduja Global Solutions, Iloilo City, Philippines　　　　　　　　Jan 2019 – Oct 2019
Healthcare Representative
- Answered calls from doctors and nurses inquiring about their patients' benefits
- Assisted customers with their complaints about their insurance.

Hyatt Centric Key West Resort and Spa, Key West, FL, USA　　　Jul 2017-Jul, 2018
Food and Beverage Trainee
- Received calls and took orders from the hotel guests and delivered them to their rooms
- Set up the bread station and coffee/water station; basic banquet set-up

Mt. Olympus Water and Theme Park, Wisconsin Dells, WI, USA　　Apr 2016 - Jun 2016
Housekeeper (Summer Work and Travel)
- Maintain all assigned areas in a clean and sanitary condition
- Responded to guests' queries and requests
- Observe and report any maintenance issues

Sea Wind Boracay Island, Aklan, Philippines　　　　　　　　　　Oct 2015 – Mar 2017
On-Call Food and Beverage Attendant
- Took orders and served food and beverages
- Attended to guests' inquiries, requests and concerns

INTERESTS

- Swimming, dancing, jogging, Zumba
- Reading, travel
- Baking, entertaining, cooking

University and Post Graduate Studies Résumé Samples

Suitable for those who have substantial education, both in their home country and in North America and seeking more permanent careers.

SUDI SHARMA

2669 West 43rd Street, Langley, BC V2Y 0B4
c. 775-784-6688, e. sharma.sudi@yahoo.ca

PROFILE

- Proficient in managing a team, specializing in motivation and team spirit
- Well-developed communication skills, customer service, and interpersonal skills
- Possesses creative problem-solving techniques; enjoys challenges
- Positive, goal-oriented, and enjoys working in a busy environment
- Sensitive to people's needs and offers empathy, motivates people to grow
- Dedicated to my work, employer and clients; upholds professional values
- Proficient in using MS Word Office
- Languages: English, Hindi, and Punjabi

EDUCATION

- **City U of Seattle in Canada,** *Bachelor of Arts in Management* | Vancouver, BC
  Intended Graduation: June 2023

- **Chandigarh University,** *Bachelor of Commerce (Hons.)* | Mohali, India
  Graduated: June 2018

EXPERIENCE

Chef and Server, *Nando's*
Langley, BC | December 2021 – present

- Preparing food, cooking, taking customer orders, serving, and cleaning tables and dishes

Assistant Accountant, *Vijay Laxmi Engineering*
Rudrapur, Uttarakhand, India | Jan 2019 – 2021

- Duties include data entry, answering phone calls, and preparing invoices
- Managing the company's accounts
- Experience with Accounting, MS Office (Word, Excel, PowerPoint)

INTERESTS

- Interacting with new people and learning about their cultures
- Hiking, travelling and exploring new places

JOHN DORY

4768 Advertick St. | Vancouver, BC V5V 5C7
778-888-7777 • jdory@me.com

PROFILE

- Specialized in Business Technology Management
- Motivated by a challenging, analytical role in technological processes or business expansion
- Natural team player with a strong desire to learn
- Displays passion for technology, sports, and business
- Exhibit excellent communication, training, and interpersonal skills
- Demonstrates behaviours of accountability, inclusive work ethics, transparency, and dependability
- Proficiency in Simply Accounting, WordPress, MS Office (Word, Excel, PowerPoint), NetSuite ERP, Stata and Internet fluency

EDUCATION

Sauder School of Business, University of British Columbia, Bachelor of Commerce
Vancouver, BC, Canada | Graduated: May 2018

- Specialization: Business Technology Management (BTM)
- Related Coursework: Introduction to Management Information Systems, Computation, Programs, and Programming

EXPERIENCE

Accounting Bookkeeper, **Light Fix Inc. of B.C.**
Richmond, BC | January 2018 – 202_

- Duties include reconciling accounts payable, and accounts receivable, data entry, preparing deposits daily and couriering to the bank, answering phone calls and preparing invoices.

Private Tutor, **Home Tutor**
Vancouver, BC | September 2013 – 2019

- Drastically improved high school and university students' grades by educating them across all subjects via explanation and guidance through difficult questions. All students achieved an 80% grade point average after months of tutoring.

Information Technology Assistant, **Vancouver College**
Vancouver, BC | September 201_ – June 201_

- Maintained the school's website, handlings confidential information, designed web pages, and was responsible for all media/technological processes for graduates.

Sales Associate, **Hometown Apparel**
Vancouver, BC | August 201_ – February 201_

- Attained the highest number of sales in my first two weeks as a result of targeting specific demographics and continuously utilizing social media effectively with a new line of clothing

EXTRACURRICULAR

Counsellor, **North Vancouver Outdoor School**
North Vancouver, BC | October 201_ – January 201_

- Garnered a greater sense of responsibility and leadership and sharpened my decision-making abilities by mentoring and managing a group of elementary students at a campsite in Squamish for a week.
- Created a safe and engaging environment for the students by leading them through activities and supervising them.

Basketball Coach, **Vancouver College**
Vancouver, BC | September 201_ – June 201_

- Coached basketball team into district champions by enhancing their skills and unravelling their potential through long, gruelling practices and intense games.
- Established greater management qualities from mentoring and developing a group of grade-seven boys.

INTERESTS

- Technology
- Basketball - Player, coach and trainer for former high schools
- Dodgeball player for UBC Intramurals Dodgeball League

Jak Willen

Vancouver, British Columbia

jak.willen@gmail.com
1 (289) 440-6789

SKILLS SUMMARY

- Proven management, problem-solving and communication skills
- Competent in using Adobe Tools and Microsoft Office applications (including MS Access)
- Highly skilled in a variety of technical operating systems, including UNIX, Linux and Windows 95/98/2000/XP/2007
- Experienced in creating HTML codes on Notepad++ and databases via Visual Basic
- Usage of domains and managing Servers such as WAMP and X-Ampp
- Competent skills in setting up computer systems (including hardware/software Installations)
- Router and switches - PC configurations and Networking
- Editing experience with video, pictures, files and presentations using Windows applications
- Creation of animations and graphics

EXPERIENCE

IBM Business Services Inc., Philippines　　　　　　　　　　　August 2018 – Present
IT Team Manager – Imaging, Configuration and Patch Management, AMTI

- Led the Desktop Engineering team that designs and builds all desktop, laptop, and tablet images for the Nationwide branches of the Bank of Philippine Islands (BPI) and UK Branches
- Deployment of Patches released officially by Microsoft and automated application installation via BigFix Tool
- Develop scripting tools to configure, manage, and support desktops, including the operating system and software application updates
- Application creation/packaging for both exe and MSI (Windows Installer)
- Basic overview training on SCCM and Desktop Central Tools

IBM Business Services Inc., AMTI, Philippines　　　　　　　　February–August 2018
Technical Support Engineer/ Helpdesk Support

- Configuration and deployment of the system units to the nationwide branches of the Bank of Philippine Islands (BPI)
- Providing technical assistance support for software, hardware and network concerns (onsite & remote) to BPI employees
- Perform routine testing and problem diagnosis while monitoring systemic service issues

EXPERIENCE (Cont'd.)

Diversified Technology Solutions International, Inc. January 2016-January, 2018
IT Engineer
- Completed 480 hours in one of the leading IT Service Management Firm, DTSI
- Excellent grading recommendation received

EDUCATION

City University of Seattle, Vancouver, Canada   Graduated: Fall, 2022

Bachelor of Arts in Management

Centro Escolar University, Philippines   Graduated: 2016

Bachelor of Science in Information Technology
Thesis: System Analysis and Design: Accessing and improving a database from a DOS-Based to Web-Based

Software Engineering: Creation of game software: Grab the Rocketeer   2015

TRAINING and SEMINARS

- Junior Philippines Computer Society
- AutoCAD Seminar
- Operating Systems and Software Installations
- Multimedia & Arts Integration Seminar

ACCOMPLISHMENTS and INTERESTS

- Homemakers Club Award
- Varsity for Basketball and Badminton
- Soccer: Two Gold Medals
- Taekwondo: Three Silver and two Bronze Medals
- Swimming: Gold and Silver Medals

Rodney Alphonso

655 Apple Street • Vancouver, British Columbia • V5R 2M5
1-345-988-1234   ralphonso@gmail.com

SKILLS SUMMARY

- Proficiency in communication (written and spoken) in English, Spanish, French, and some Italian
- Creative problem-solving, competent in handling complex communications, translation
- Multi-cultural background; excels in collaboration, service, and communication
- Adept in time management, team leadership and interpersonal skills
- Highly developed organization skills, event and exhibition planning, and detail-oriented
- Educated awareness of global issues and needs; passionate about education and helping others
- Expertise in fine arts, travelling worldwide, working with high-profile professionals and royalty
- Computer software knowledge and use: Microsoft Office, Internet, social media; proficiency in Adobe Cloud Software: Premiere, InDesign, Illustrator, and Spark

PROFESSIONAL and VOLUNTEER EXPERIENCE

Catlett Law Firm – Vancouver, BC   January 2020 – Present
Legal Art Assistant
- Responsible for art selections for display, distribution for Museum art events, and verification of copywritten and intellectual property of all artwork.

University of Arkansas of Medical Science – Little Rock, AR   May 2020
Volunteer/Translator
- Provided English/Spanish translations to medical workers and police regarding people getting their temperatures checked for COVID 19

Clinton Library – Little Rock, AR   April – September 2020
Volunteer/Meal distribution
- Assisted in World Central Kitchen packaging food, checking inventory, disinfecting areas and loading food trucks to donate to those affected by COVID 19

Wings of Hope – Stillwater, Oklahoma   August 2018 – May 2019
Volunteer Translator
- Translator for local law enforcement dealing with cases of family abuse

Crossroads Foundation Ltd. – Hong Kong   June – August 2018
Intern For a non-profit organization serving global needs
- Organized inventory of donated goods in the worldwide shipping department
- Trained and instructed new interns
- Created and edited video content in the communication department
- Coordinated with other departments for the preparation of international shipping

General Consulate of Mexico – San Antonio, Texas, USA   June – August 2018
Consular Officer
- Collaborate in the organization of cultural and official events
- Organized meetings for legal procedures
- Granted Mexican citizenships, processed passports, birth certificates

Oklahoma State University – Stillwater, OK   August 2017 – May 2019
Graduate Assistant
- Prepared events for guest speakers, including the former First Minister of Scotland, Prince of Ethiopia, and other diplomatic figures
- Created the database for the Memorandum of Understandings with International universities
- Proposed ideas for renovating the hallways of the Global Studies and Partnerships building and provided posters from the Museum of Anthropology of Mexico City

EDUCATION

City University of Seattle Vancouver, BC, Canada
    BA in Management – Graduated   December 2021

Oklahoma State University, OK
    Masters In Global Studies. - Graduated   May 2019

Universidad De Monterrey, MX
    Bachelors In International Studies. - Graduated   November 2014

NOTE:

The following résumé was done through an ATS App that many students use called an Applicant Tracking System. It is the same résumé as this one; however, the format is different. Many recruiters in Canada and the US use these APPs to scan the résumés quickly and to look for key words for qualifications and skills.

The drawback, based on my research, is that a human won't read a paragraph, which replaced the bulleted Profile. I prefer to have all your best skills, technical and soft skills, as well as languages in the Profile or Skills Summary.

The format provided by these APPS is in multiple tables which makes it extremely difficult to edit or add other information.

The APPs charge a nominal fee for every document you create.

Rodney Alphonso
655 Apple Street • Vancouver, British Columbia • V5R 2M5
1-345-988-1234   ralphonso@gmail.com

PROFILE

Reliable candidate ready to take on challenges using problem-solving, critical thinking and task prioritization skills to help the team succeed. A servant leader who cares about diversity, inclusion and equality by supporting the client and the organization. Spoken languages include English, Spanish, French and some Italian. Technical and software skills in MS Office, Adobe Cloud, Premiere, InDesign, Illustrator, and Spark.

SKILLS

- Critical thinking, problem solving, and conflict resolution
- Excels in organization, event planning, and details
- Competent in team leadership and interpersonal skills
- Facilitates effective and efficient team meetings

WORK EXPERIENCE

Catlett Law Firm | Little Rock, AR   January 2020 - July 2021
Legal Art Assistant
Responsible for art selections for display, distribution to: Museum art events, verification of copywritten and intellectual property of an artwork

University of Arkansas of Medical Science | Little Rock, AR   May 2020
Translator Volunteer

Provided English/Spanish translations to medical workers and police regarding people getting their temperatures checked for COVID 19

Clinton Library | Little Rock, AR   April - September 2020
COVID-19 Meal Distribution Volunteer

- Assisted in World Central Kitchen packaging food, checking inventory, disinfecting areas and loading food trucks to donate to those affected by COVID 19

Wings of Hope | Stillwater, Oklahoma   August 2018 - May 2019
Translator

- Translator for local law enforcement whenever there were cases of family abuse

Crossroads Foundation Ltd. | Hong Kong
Intern for Global Needs Non-Profit June - August 2018
- Responsible for organizing the inventory of donated goods; coordinated international shipping with other departments and ensured all freight containers were loaded properly
- Trained all new interns
- Created an edited video for the communications department

General Consulate of Mexico | San Antonio, Texas, USA June - August 2018
Consular Officer
- Collaborated to organize all cultural and official events
- Organized legal procedure meetings
- Granted Mexican citizenships; located and printed birth certificates, passports

Oklahoma State University | Stillwater, OK August 2017 - May 2019
Graduate Assistant
- Prepared events for guest speakers, including the former First Minister of Scotland, Prince of Ethiopia, and other diplomatic figures; assisted in academic and cultural exhibitions
- Created the database for the Memorandum of Understandings with International universities
- Organized inventory in the building of Global Studies and Partnerships; proposed and implemented renovation ideas

EDUCATION

City U of Seattle in Canada, Vancouver, BC Canada
BA in Management December 2021

Oklahoma State University, Stillwater, OK
MA Global Studies May 2019

Universidad de Monterrey, Nuevo Leon, Mexico
BA International Studies November 2014

LANGUAGES

English   Spanish   French   Italian

DALAPATHI (DAL) SINGH

6770 Victoria Drive, Vancouver, BC V8D 1G3
Email: dal.singh@gmail.com
Mobile: 1 (778) 699-8885

SKILLS SUMMARY

- Highly developed proficiency in managing a team, specializing in motivation and team spirit
- Demonstrates excellent communication skills, customer service
- Possesses creative problem-solving techniques; enjoys challenges
- Positive, goal-oriented, and enjoys working in a busy environment
- Sensitive to people's needs; highly empathetic, helps people grow
- Proficiency in MS Word Office, Internet
- Languages: written and spoken English and Punjabi

EDUCATION

City U of Seattle (Canada), Vancouver, BC
Bachelor of Arts in Management — Graduated Fall, 2022

NTEC Christchurch, New Zealand — 2016 – 2017
Diploma in Business Management, Level 6

NTEC, Tauranga, New Zealand — 2015 – 2016
Diploma in Business Management Level 5

EMPLOYMENT HISTORY

BC LIQUOR, Vancouver, BC — December 2020 - present
Store Manager
Responsible for opening the store, onboarding new staff, and product knowledge. Excels at customer service, special event promotions, financial tracking, and strategic planning.

New World Supermarket, Kaikoura, New Zealand — July 2017 – November 2020
Liquor Manager — (2018-2020)
Managed all staff in a busy liquor store, offering excellent customer service, ordering inventory, special event orders, financial tracking, and quality control.

Countdown South Ashburton, NZ — May – July 2017
Night Supervisor
Responsible for supervising teams, achieving financial sales targets, and filling alcohol promotional and special event orders.

La Brioche Patisserie, Tauranga, NZ — October– December 2015
Duties included kitchen team support, delivery driver, and excellent customer service

ISABELLA GARCIA

238 E. Metabello Drive
Kelowna, BC V1W 1G4
M. 250-887-8989   E. garcia.bella@me.com

SKILLS SUMMARY

- Specialized in supporting children with spectrum disorders, such as Asperger's and ADHD
- Highly creative and experienced teacher and coach with young students 3 - 11 years of age
- Demonstrates positive energy, remaining calm in challenging situations and maintaining a happy, respectful environment for the children
- Demonstrates organization in time management, activity planning and creating a calm atmosphere
- Innovative and flexible in developing change based on the current needs of my young clients
- Dynamic and enthusiastic when creating new activities that produce joy and fun
- Dedicated, loyal, artistic, creative, flexible

EDUCATION AND TRAINING

BA in Management
City U of Seattle (in Canada) Vancouver, BC. Graduated   Spring, 2023

Standard First Aid Training
Level C CPR/AED Vancouver, BC. Graduated   2022

Workshop Socio-environmental Management for Energy,
Universidad Politecnica del Centro, MX. Graduated   2019

Ph.D. Education
Universidad Abierta de Tlaxcala, Tlaxcala, MX. Graduated   2018

Spanish Certification
Teaching as a Foreign Language Instituto Hemingway, MX   2015

MA Innovation and Educational Technology
Instituto de Estudios Universitarios (IEU) Tabasco, MX   2013

EMPLOYMENT AND VOLUNTEER EXPERIENCE

Nanny   **Self-Employed**, Vancouver, BC
2021-present   Responsible for twin boys to engage them in activities, routines, educational and cognitive development

Online Tutor   **Self-Employed**, Vancouver, BC
2006-present   Assisting children with homework, studies and personal achievement

Professor 2018-2022	**Universidad Politecnica del Centro**, Tabasco, MX Taught English, French, professional ethics and writing to university students
Teacher 2015-2017	**Colegio Tabasco de Varones**, Tabasco, MX Taught English to high school students, grades one to three
Teacher 2015-2017	**Colegio Tabasco de Varones**, Tabasco, MX Taught English as ESL to children, ages 2 to 6 years of age
Dept. Head Primary Teacher 2010 – 2015	**Instituto Cumbres Villahermosa**, Tabasco, MX Department leader for all teachers offering English classes in English, science, language arts, and social studies
Soccer Coach 2011-2012	**Instituto Cumbres Villahermosa**, Tabasco, MX Coached children ages 6- 10 years.
Au Pair August 2013-July 2014	**Intercultural Exchange**, Paris, FR Responsible for three children (ages 6, 8, and 11) while living in France.

ACCOMPLISHMENTS

- **Speaker**: *International Congress of Pedagogy*, La Habana, Cuba, 2019
  Topic: Adaptation of the UPC student to the BIS model (bilingual, international and sustainability)

- **Speaker:** *IX International Congress of Environmental Education for Sustainability*, Mazatlán, Sinaloa, Mexico, 2019. Topic: "Restoration of the Aquatic System"

- **Co-author of the article**: "Solar heat applied to heating food by automating a closed cycle of the International Research Congress Academia Journals" Hidalgo, México, 2019

INTERESTS AND COMMUNITY INVOLVEMENT

- Sports, movies, travel, pop culture, child development

- Ambassador WeXplore studies agency in Mexico with a presence in Vancouver, B.C.

DEVEN BRAR

4555 Aristotle Drive, Calgary, AB T1E 7S1
Email: cbrar@gmail.com • Mobile: 1 (228) 681-0944

SKILLS SUMMARY

- Proficient in managing a team, specializing in motivation and team spirit
- Highly developed communication skills, customer service
- Possesses creative problem-solving techniques; enjoys challenges
- Positive, goal-oriented, and enjoys working in a busy environment
- Sensitive to people's needs, offer empathy and help people grow
- Proficient in MS Word Office, Excel, and POS to place orders
- Languages: English, Punjabi, and Hindi

EDUCATION

City U of Seattle (Canada), Calgary, BC Spring 2023
Bachelor of Business and Management. Graduated.

NTEC Christchurch, New Zealand 2016 – 2017
Diploma in Business Management, Level 6

NTEC, Tauranga, New Zealand 2015 – 2016
Diploma in Business Management Level 5

EMPLOYMENT HISTORY

U-Brew Plus, Calgary, BC September 2022 - Present
Liquor Assistant
Greeting and helping customers with their queries, handling cash daily, restocking shelves, receiving deliveries, promoting products, and maintaining a clean and presentable store

Apex Liquor Market, Calgary, BC October 2021- September 2022
Liquor Assistant
Handling cash daily, sales, handling customer conflicts, filling alcohol, and receiving deliveries

New World Supermarket, Kaikoura, New Zealand July 2017 – November 2020
Liquor Manager *(2018-2020)*
Full responsibility for managing all staff in a busy liquor department, offering excellent customer service, conducting regular inventory checks, ordering special event orders, financial tracking, dealing with suppliers, monitoring sales and implementing various strategies to increase revenue and quality control.

Countdown South Ashburton, NZ May – July 2017
Night Supervisor
Responsible for supervising teams, achieving financial sales targets, and filling alcohol promotional and special event orders.

La Brioche Pâtisserie, Tauranga, NZ October – December 2015
Duties included kitchen team support, delivery driver, and excellent customer service

INTERESTS

- Playing and watching soccer; hiking
- Fascinated with learning diverse languages
- Exploring the natural beauty of the environment through hiking
- Capturing the uniqueness of nature's surroundings through photography
- Experimenting and learning about photography and cameras

Chapter Seven

COVER LETTERS AND FOLLOW-UP LETTERS

Over time, we have lost the art of letter writing. Since most people now use texting and emailing to communicate, our traditional writing skills have decreased significantly. Many people don't write cover or thank you letters, yet it is a skill that is still appreciated and may be the deciding factor whether you advance in the job-finding process. Some examples will follow, no matter how "rusty" you may be.

Letters of Importance in the Job-finding Process

- Cover letter (to accompany your résumé)
- Cover letter based on a referral for the job
- General cover letter to introduce yourself
- Thank you note for the interview
- I'm still interested letter…
- Letter of acceptance
- Letter after a rejection
- Turning down a job offer
- Leaving a job

The Cover Letter

There's much controversy about whether a cover letter is required for the selection process, especially when it is sent electronically through an Internet application. Some employers will skim your letter quickly, looking for keywords such as roles, skills, and accomplishments, while others prefer the content in the cover letter over the résumé to gain a better understanding of the applicant, their qualifications and desire to work for the employer.

Learning the art of crafting a compelling cover letter is a must for every applicant. Employers look through cover letters to learn about the skills you can offer and gain more insight into your personality. Your cover letter needs to be exciting and should consist of no less than three and no more than five paragraphs. The letter is written specifically for *each* job application and is the gateway to reading the résumé. If employers want you only to submit a résumé, I suggest you have the letter accompanying the résumé in the same file. Save the documents as a PDF.

Each letter must be supported by your best skills and experiences that relate directly to each job. Ensure that the descriptors that you use are also from the advertisement. For example, use those exact words in your letter if they want specific skills such as experience with tools or organization skills. Many companies will use scanners for both the letter and résumé to seek keywords to pre-select their applicants.

In the letter, you will:

- Address a specific person who will read the letter. This extra effort (phoning the company or researching the company on the Internet) may move you up the ladder of consideration.

- State why you are interested in the position.

- Describe your strengths, interests and skills related to the job that you can offer the company

- Describe your relevant experience and how that will benefit them.

- Ask for an interview, and tell them when and where you can be contacted.

Five Basic Paragraphs of Letter Writing

The following five basic paragraphs will apply to all types of letters (business or friendly), regardless of whom you are writing or for what purpose. A cover letter for a position should be no more than one page long; it should be concise and say only what is necessary to entice the reader to respond favourably. The letter should be between three and five paragraphs. A personal letter can be longer than a page. Don't forget that the purpose of a cover letter is to get you to the next step, and in a job search, you want an interview!

Basic Information for Letters of All Kinds

Examples of Letters	Cover Letter for Employment	Letter of Complaint (Regarding a service or product)	Invitation Letter or friendly letter
Paragraph One Will contain the reason WHY you are writing	I am applying for the position you advertised. Describe the job specifically and accurately.	I want to complain about a dishwasher, Model 1324B from your store.	I'd like to invite you to visit over the summer.
Paragraph Two Information qualifying your reason for writing	State and describe that you qualify for the position.	Describe the item that you are complaining about and what appears to be the problem.	Give details of the invitation (July 14-25 at Whistler, BC)
Paragraph Three Contains unique information regarding the topic	Relay something that you can offer that might be considered unique. It should relate to the job requirements.	Give specific information about the defective product. (Model, price, date of purchase)	Tell a bit about what you will do on the visit. (Kayaking, swimming, heli-skiing)
Paragraph Four-Five: State what you want the reader to do now	Ask them to contact you for an interview. A polite closing and thank you. State that you will follow up with them within the next 5-10 business days.	Replace or repair the product (or refund my money). A polite closing and thank you. State that you will follow up with them within the next 5-10 business days.	Write or phone me to let me know you are coming and how/what time I can pick you up. A polite closing and thank you. State that you will follow up with them within the next 5-10 days.

Selling Yourself: What's Your Personal Brand?

Most of us have heard of businesses with a brand or logo that creates an "image" when we think about that business or product/service. It is not necessarily based on a company's vision or mission statement but rather on a person's perspective of the product, services or company's image, determining whether they like or dislike that brand for their own use. When a candidate is seeking a job, you must create your own personal brand (before someone else determines your brand for you).

Personal branding is about being recognized as unique and the best fit for a job. It's about how well you sell yourself. You will want to give yourself a competitive advantage over other candidates and learning how to demonstrate your unique combination of skills, strengths, and experiences can set you apart from others.

Branding includes a number of characteristics that will command respect and confidence from your peers and recruiters. How people see you involves many attributes and includes the following:

- Your personal image, how you dress, walk and talk, and your personality characteristics

- How well you portray your strengths, skills, recognizable behaviours and values

- How well you have researched the company and the recruiter, answered the interview questions, and followed up with a thank you letter

No matter how professional it may sound, selling yourself will not be accomplished by writing an email like the one I received: *"I have the great skills you want. I have numerous experiences and a proven track record of performance."* To be honest, I didn't go any further with this applicant, as this was far from my idea of a cover letter.

When you're looking for a new job, you're a marketer. You're the "product," and you need to use your résumé, a professional LinkedIn profile, a cover letter, and any other materials to engage and influence people. Hopefully, they will want to contact you and hire you right away. Some people create websites that describe their values and professional profile. The website must be clear, concise and look professional. Study other people's profiles and websites of others with a personal or LinkedIn profile to learn how to write a good profile.

Your letter must be professional to get the reader's attention and interest. The art to all this lies in captivating your audience in creative, engaging, and original ways — without going over the top or coming off as nonsensical.

How do you pull this off? Here are examples that will show you the critical difference:

What's boring? This is…

> *To Whom It May Concern,*
>
> *I am responding to your August 12th advertisement for a Senior Analyst. I am uniquely qualified for this role.*

This is better.

Dear Mr. Martins:

> *My love of reaching goals and problem-solving dates back to age twelve. I will always be grateful that I had a clear goal that required planning, persistence, problem-solving and a lifetime goal. I had no idea these qualities would lead me to a career in serving corporate clients and problem-solving. My talents could serve XYZ company very well. Here's how…*

Starting a cover letter with a "hook" or a statement that draws the reader into your story piques their interest and draws them in to read more about your qualifications. Most people enjoy reading about your story.

Tips to Make Your Letter Awesome!

- Refer to the specific job that you are interested in. If there is a competition number, include it.

- Address your letter to the appropriate contact person, the employer or a human resources manager. Use their name and title, and double-check the spelling. And don't assume a person is male or female—check it out! Phone the company, Google the HR manager or look on their business website for a list of managers. Even if it is not the person who will be reading your resume, you have taken the initiative to search for a relevant person in HR.

- Refer to how you heard about the job—a newspaper ad, a sign in the window, from a friend, or an online job app such as Indeed.com, Glassdoor.com, SimplyHired.com, LinkedIn.com,

ZipRecruiter.com, WorkBC.ca, or BetterTeam.com. If you mention a current employee who recommended you apply for this job, make sure you know that <u>they</u> are considered a valued employee!

- Perhaps mention the company's purpose or industry and how your attributes can benefit their team.

- Ensure the employer knows what action to take—should they expect you to call them, or should he/she contact you—and when? Always ask for an appointment for an interview.

- Provide your name, address, phone number, and email address.

- Keep your letter to one page, typed and single-spaced. Print it on good quality, letter-size paper 8 ½ x 11 inches (21.5 x 27.9 cm) if you are mailing or delivering it. Try not to use photocopy paper, but rather something a bit heavier.

- Proofread your letter, and ask someone else to read it as well. It must be error-free and grammatically correct.

- Most applications are requested online, but if you can hand-deliver your application for a better "first impression," do it. Remember to dress as if you were going to have an interview. Be prepared in case that happens!

- Save your complete application (letter and résumé) in your computer files and save a record of the companies you've applied to. You'll find a form to record the companies later in this book.

Allow plenty of time for delivery. Don't wait until the last day before a deadline. If you have Internet problems at the last minute, you may not get your application in on time.

The next section offers sample letters suitable for a person entering the workplace and beyond. Even if you are applying for a seat in a college program or have some workplace experience, you can quickly adapt your letters to suit your needs. The proper format and spacing for a letter come first. Below is a sample cover letter with the suggested spacing so that your letter appears balanced on the page and is attractively presented. Like everything else, your letter can create a great first impression and indicates that you have good attention to detail and care enough to ensure it is error-free and easy to read.

When carefully written, your cover letter should leave a hiring manager with a positive and memorable impression of you -- something a résumé alone won't always do. In the following template, the words in [brackets] can be replaced with information about yourself and the reason(s) for your application. Modify any of the pre-written sections to ensure it's a personalized cover letter.

Once you're ready to begin, copy the template, paste it onto Microsoft Word or a new Google doc, save it as its own file, and send it to the companies you are applying to. I also suggest you save and send each cover letter as a PDF file. Write your last name on the file and the position and date as references.
(E.g., Chan.ABCProjectmgr_10_2023.pdf).

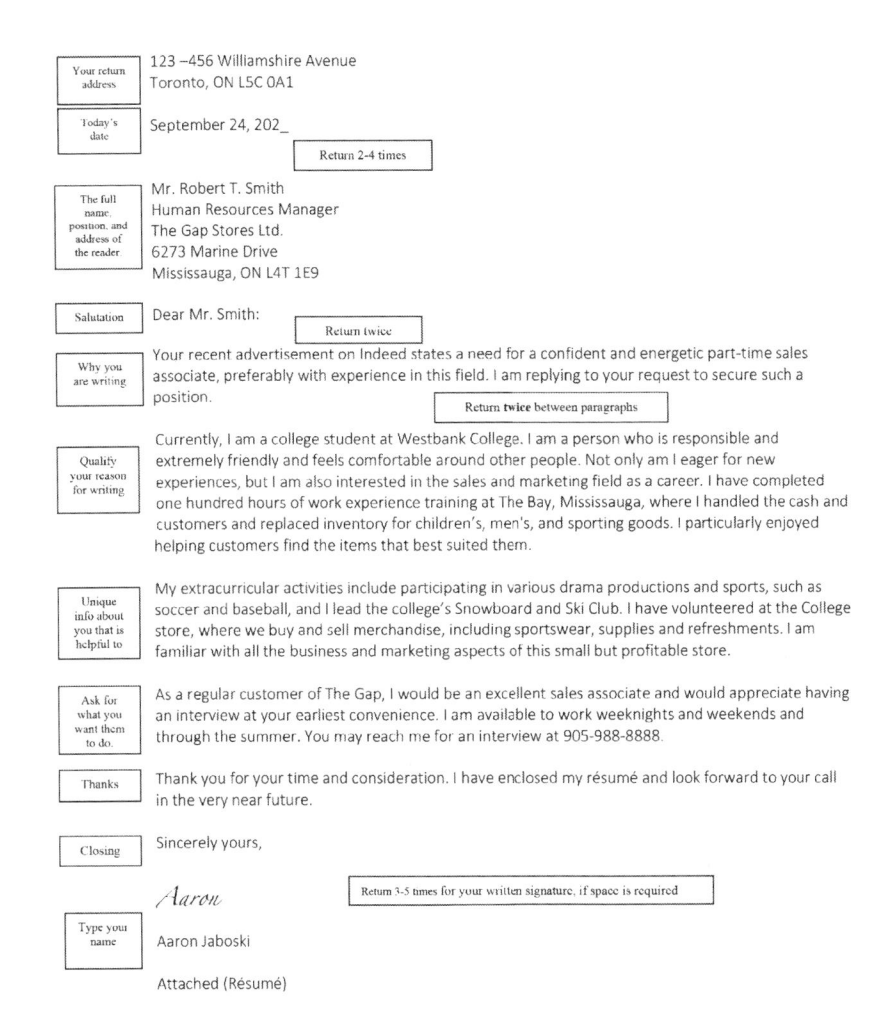

Your return address	123 –456 Williamshire Avenue Toronto, ON L5C 0A1
Today's date	September 24, 202_

Return 2-4 times

The full name, position, and address of the reader	Mr. Robert T. Smith Human Resources Manager The Gap Stores Ltd. 6273 Marine Drive Mississauga, ON L4T 1E9
Salutation	Dear Mr. Smith:

Return twice

Why you are writing	Your recent advertisement on Indeed states a need for a confident and energetic part-time sales associate, preferably with experience in this field. I am replying to your request to secure such a position.

*Return **twice** between paragraphs*

Qualify your reason for writing	Currently, I am a college student at Westbank College. I am a person who is responsible and extremely friendly and feels comfortable around other people. Not only am I eager for new experiences, but I am also interested in the sales and marketing field as a career. I have completed one hundred hours of work experience training at The Bay, Mississauga, where I handled the cash and customers and replaced inventory for children's, men's, and sporting goods. I particularly enjoyed helping customers find the items that best suited them.
Unique info about you that is helpful to	My extracurricular activities include participating in various drama productions and sports, such as soccer and baseball, and I lead the college's Snowboard and Ski Club. I have volunteered at the College store, where we buy and sell merchandise, including sportswear, supplies and refreshments. I am familiar with all the business and marketing aspects of this small but profitable store.
Ask for what you want them to do.	As a regular customer of The Gap, I would be an excellent sales associate and would appreciate having an interview at your earliest convenience. I am available to work weeknights and weekends and through the summer. You may reach me for an interview at 905-988-8888.
Thanks	Thank you for your time and consideration. I have enclosed my résumé and look forward to your call in the very near future.
Closing	Sincerely yours,

Aaron

Return 3-5 times for your written signature, if space is required

Type your name	Aaron Jaboski

Attached (Résumé)

Remember to tailor your letter to **each** company and job. You can NOT send the same letter to every company's advertisement. I once received a cover letter addressed to me, but it clearly was a letter applying for a job at a different company. I never even glanced at their résumé.

I was amazed at the difference it made when I tested out the reaction I got from potential employers when I used some of the phrases from my StrengthsFinder/ Now, Discover Your Strengths assessment. Within two weeks, I sent out eight applications. Four had the usual wording that was professional and explanatory. The other four had specific phrases from my StrengthsFinder's description of what I could offer the company based on my strengths. Within a few days, I received responses from all four applications where I used my personal Strengths phrases. Recently, Amazon has listed the latest version of this book, *"Now, Discover Your Strengths,"* and contains an updated version of the StrengthsFinder 2.0 assessment. Just remember to "check" that the envelope at the back of the book is present and unopened, as the code enclosed can only be used once.

As a result, I had four interviews and was offered a job after a thorough interview. I wanted that job as it aligned with my goals and values perfectly. Even though I am self-assured and am usually very confident during interviews, I still practiced and prepared for the interviews. Although the panel interview was via Zoom, I set up my computer, the lighting, and the background an hour before the interview. I tested all my technology and opened Zoom to check that the lighting, background and sound were perfect. I chose an outfit that suited my colouring and then printed the documents I might need as quick references. In addition, I reviewed my answers to many interview questions I had answered in my "JOB PREP" book. (Yes, I have a journal with all the answers to various behaviour questions, with multiple answers for each question). I was set to "wow" them, and apparently, I did! You will never know who your competition is for the job, and preparation, professionalism, and practice will not only let you feel more confident, but you may have a much better chance of being offered that ideal job. Preparation yields confidence.

Sample Letters

In the following pages, you will find a selection of letters that address your letter-writing needs, including:

Templates

General Introduction Letter

Entry-level Positions

University Graduates

Post-graduation

Cover Letter

Thank You Letters

Rejection Follow-up Letter

Cover Letter Template

(Your Name)
(Street Address) | (City, Province, Postal Code) | (Email Address) | (Phone Number)

Hiring Manager's Name
Position
Company Name
Street Address
City, Province/State, Postal/Zip code

Dear [Hiring Manager]:

I am excited to apply for the [position] role at [Company]. As an international student, I am eager to gain experience in my field of study and contribute to your company's growth.

I have developed a strong foundation in [skill/industry] throughout my academic career. I can apply this knowledge to [task/responsibility] in the [position] role. My experience at a [previous job/internship] has allowed me to develop my [skills/industry] skills and work collaboratively with diverse teams.

One of my strengths is my ability to adapt quickly to new environments. As an international student, I understand the importance of flexibility and adaptability. I am excited to apply these skills to the dynamic and ever-changing work environment at [company].

I am particularly impressed with [company values/mission statement]. I am excited about joining such an impressive and innovative team.

Thank you for considering my application. I am keen to discuss how I can contribute to the growth and success of [company].

Sincerely,

Your name

General Letter of Introduction

Marta Giuseppe
Apt. 52 – 89787 Wilkins Street
Kitchener, ON N2A 0A4
m. 226-812-9954   e. martaG@yahoo.ca

September 14, 202_

Human Resources Department
Delivered by Hand

Dear Sir or Madam:

RE: Letter of Introduction

I want to introduce myself, as I am an international student at [university] studying [state the area of study] and am interested in applying my skills of organization, time management, attention to detail and customer service to a Canadian business, such as yours, on a part-time basis.

My background in the Philippines has been working for a real estate company for the past six years, and I am eager to adapt to the Canadian workforce while studying. Even though my enclosed résumé demonstrates my experiences and capabilities, I lack knowledge of the differences between my work in Manilla and in Canada. That's where we might be able to help each other. I realize that many of the jobs for a "new arrival" will be less challenging than my previous work, but the challenge will be to learn how to do all tasks properly from your point of view. I am eager to learn to prove my value to you and your teams.

While attending university, I have available hours to work without interrupting my study schedule. I want to discuss what areas where you can use my skills of dedication, quick learning, and customer service during the days of Tuesday and Wednesday and the evenings of Thursday and Friday. If you require my assistance on the weekends, I am available on Saturday.

I have enclosed my résumé for your perusal and hope you will reach out by email or phone to arrange an interview so we can discuss how I might add to your productivity.

I'll look forward to hearing from you. I also have your contact information from your reception desk and will connect with you within the week to ensure that you received my letter and résumé. Thank you for your time and consideration.

Sincerely,

Marta

Marta Giuseppe
Enclosure

Entry Level Cover Letter

1234 Mountain Street
North Vancouver, BC V5G 1T4

March 24, 202__

Mr. T. McMasters
Smith's Tae Kwon Do Studios
123 Lonsdale Avenue
North Vancouver, BC V6G 2A2

Dear Mr. McMasters:

Job Posting # 5048-12

I am writing regarding your need for a computer-managing assistant position which I saw in your March 15th posting in Indeed. My combined love and knowledge of computers, technology and martial arts should qualify me for this position, and I would appreciate your consideration.

I am studying Kinesthetics and business in my first year at Capilano University in North Vancouver. I am eager to fill this position related to Martial Arts, where I earned Level 3 Dan, Tae Kwon Do certification in Korea. In addition, I am currently attending Smith's Martial Arts as a client to learn the possible differences in Canadian styles. You will find me a tenacious and enthusiastic person who can manage all the duties associated with the student roster and the website. Apart from my profound interest in Tae Kwon Do, I achieved excellent grades in Information Technology during my first year at CAP U. I was among the few students who created the North Shore Secondary School website. These collective traits indicate how I would be suited to the position of computer-managing assistant.

I am fluent in English and Korean; you will find me responsible and hard-working. In the four years that I have been in Canada, I have been involved in many extra-curricular activities, including a piloted business venture at our school, where I served as the Vice President of Finance. I managed to complete both Grades 11 and 12 in one year and have been the recipient of several business and accounting awards.

My experiences outlined in the attached resume have sharpened my abilities to accomplish new tasks, and I look forward to working with your team. I will contact you within seven business days to arrange a suitable time for an interview. Thank you for your time and consideration. I look forward to meeting with you.

Sincerely yours,

Joon Luck

Joon Luck
778-898-4000

Enclosure

Internship Letter of Application

1234 South Bend Avenue
North Vancouver, BC
V7K 2L5

March 26, 202_

Mr. Charles Hansen
Production Manager
ABL Television Studio Ltd.
Ste. 2070 - One West Monroe Street
Vancouver, BC V8K 2C4

Dear Mr. Hansen:

<u>RE: Summer Internship Position</u>

I am writing to request the opportunity to work as a summer intern for you. My BCIT career advisor, Mr. James Smythe, suggested your firm, as you often take on student interns from May through August.

I am a third-year applied communications student at BCIT in Burnaby. My ultimate goal is to enter the field of communication, particularly TV or radio broadcasting. I plan to use my summer to learn and apply more about the intricacies of media production. I am willing to begin at an entry-level position to familiarize myself with as many departments as possible.

As the enclosed resume indicates, I am a hard worker who takes pride in doing the best possible job at whatever task I take on. My favourite studies include organizational communications (writing and public speaking) and radio and TV broadcasting. I am competent with both Apple and PC systems.

I want to arrange a time to visit you at your convenience to learn more about how I can contribute my abilities to your studio and employees. My cell phone number is 604-123-4566. I appreciate your consideration and will follow up next week by telephone to discuss arrangements to meet with you.

Sincerely,

Paulo Ruiz
Enclosure

Cover Letter Based on a Referral

(Your Name)
(Street Address)
(City, Province, Postal Code)
(Email Address) | (Phone Number)

(Date)

(Hiring Manager's Name)
Intel Production Ltd.
(Street Address)
(City, Province, Postal Code)

Dear (Hiring Manager's Name):

My former business associate and a close friend, Eric Mathers, VP of Production at your company, suggested I contact you regarding the Project Manager position you want to fill. Eric flagged this opportunity for me upon realizing that my project management experience aligns seamlessly with the qualifications for the opportunity at hand.

After working as an assistant project manager for Maple Leaf Systems (MLS) Ltd. for four years, I am ready to transition into a position that presents an exciting new set of challenges. While my time at MLS has led me to career milestones such as meeting critical deadlines for two lengthy projects, developing quick problem-solving methods for unusual dilemmas, and creating a highly productive team, I'm excited by Intel Production's need for meeting deadlines and problem-solving during critical situations. I feel confident that my ability to handle these skills would enable me to ramp up quickly in this position to begin making an impact soon.

For more information regarding my qualifications, please review my attached resume. I would greatly appreciate an opportunity to discuss this position in more detail and would appreciate discussing a convenient time for us to meet.

Thank you for considering my application.

Sincerely,

(Your signature)

Type Your name

University Graduate Cover Letter

1109 – 1327 E. Keith Road
Winnipeg, MB R2C 0G8

July 12, 202_

One-Right Solutions
Human Resources Manager
4559 First Avenue, 6th Floor
Winnipeg, MB R2W 2M5

EMAILED: info@onerightsolutions.com

Dear Sir or Madam:

RE: HR Training Advisor

With a career base of training, management, leadership, curriculum design and implementation, it is with great anticipation that I apply for this position. I have been assessing the training needs of adults (and youth) for over 15 years, leading them to a place where they have been engaged, excited, and focused on their development and training. I have extensive experience working with executives, employees, supervisors and stakeholders of all ages.

In the attached detailed resume, you will note that my background is diversified. Whether I work for a large organization or my own business, my love of servicing others is paramount. I have abundant energy, experience, and a desire to continue engaging others for high performance in their lives and careers. I am a leader of teams and have been told that I am gifted in creating and applying unique training initiatives that provide motivation, engagement, and progress.

Through my business, I assisted numerous managers and organizations in developing a highly productive culture, multi-generational teams and engaged collaboration. My passion for seeing the potential of others and those who teach and advise them motivates me to develop creative ways to excite and engage people in learning, growing, and succeeding. I enjoy a challenge and am highly organized in project management, collaboration, and development.

I have a keen sense of humour and excellent interpersonal skills, which allow me to engage and build rapport with people of all ages. I have enjoyed speaking to HR managers, business leaders and owners about employee retention and motivation topics.

I'd appreciate you perusing my enclosed documents and connecting with me for an interview to discuss your needs and my qualifications further. I can be reached by the contacts below, and I look forward to your call. I appreciate your consideration.

Sincerely,

Alfonso López

University Graduate Cover Letter

CHRISTINE ORESKOVIC
18 West First Avenue Vancouver, BC • V6J 0B3 • 604 778 5333 • kikioreskovich@gmail.com

March 23, 202_

Lululemon Athletica Ltd.
Human Resources
1818 Cornwall Avenue
Vancouver, BC V6J 1C7

On-Line Application

To Whom It May Concern:

RE: RETAIL TRAINING MANAGER: CANADA

As your potential Retail Training Manager, I would like to bring my past experience and desire for growth and excitement to your company. Some attributes I will bring to Lululemon include energy, tenacity and dedication, and personal and career-based visions.

My attached resume shows that my extensive sales and business management experience over the past twelve years will augment my leadership skills, which can easily transfer to the Retail Training Manager position. The people I have previously supervised and trained have developed successful careers and client relations, and I continue to motivate those with whom I work.

I am a positive person who has the capability to read people's motivations easily and can bring creative ideas to communicate and help implement their goals with those of the company. I am a true leader; I radiate authenticity, concern, and altruism for others. Building relationships with the sales team and directors is key in leading the charge, uniting and motivating my team with my infectious enthusiasm. I have always admired the core values of Lululemon. I will continue to celebrate and embody your reputation to approach your staff with personal development training and encourage them to take on personal, authentic leadership.

The credentials and attitudes that you require for this important position are those that I possess. I would greatly appreciate an opportunity to expand on my qualifications in an interview at your convenience. I believe there is no match for your product quality and corporate integrity, and I can't think of another organization where I would prefer to work. Thank you for your time and consideration. I'll look forward to your reply.

Sincerely,

Christine

Christine Oreskovic

University Graduate Cover Letter

MARTA GARCÍA
589 Seymour Street • Vancouver, B.C. V6G 3M1 • m. 604-877-7889

September 27, 202_

Mr. B. Jonas
HR Manager
Elental Foundation Corp.
Ste. 1808 – 900 Columbia Street
New Westminster, BC V9J 4C8

Sent by Email: jonasb@elental.com

Dear Mr. Jonas:

RE: Job Position Number: NH 4226

My interest in the Fundraising Coordinator position was piqued when I read your advertisement in Indeed, as I have previous experience as a Fundraising Coordinator and loved that job. I am self-motivated and have developed and executed strategies to bring valuable fundraising results to the Elental Foundation.

With my ability and love for learning, I can quickly adapt to your policies and procedures to become an asset to your team. My effective communication skills and the motivation to take on challenging work have allowed me to fine-tune leadership, teamwork, and empathy. Being confident, I have developed the drive and enthusiasm that would be a great addition to your team. Previously, I handled various responsibilities and quickly established prioritizing tasks, meeting deadlines and finding solutions to eliminate obstacles.

As a recent graduate from City University of Seattle in Vancouver, BC, I seek new challenges and to collaborate with a fresh team of talented professionals. I relish the opportunity to improve operations and seek better methods to achieve more reliable and faster results for Elental.

Leaving my country to become educated in Canada allowed me to build strong connections with other individuals and cultures, cultivating new growth and a better understanding of my future goals.

I am available for an interview at your convenience and look forward to discussing your needs and how my qualifications may fit your team and goals.

Sincerely,

Marta García

Attached: resume

Letter Requesting Consideration for a More Senior Role

Ste. 311 – 4546 West 54 Avenue
Kitchener, ON N2G 1G4

March 14, 202_

Their full names (first and last)
Company Name
Mailing Address
City, ON Postal Code

Dear Deni and Nicola:

RE: Consideration for a more senior role

As you may know, I hold a study permit while attending the University of Waterloo and will graduate with a BA in Business Administration by December 202_. Shortly after, I will have my PGWP (two-to-three work permit). I would like to know if you will consider me for a team lead or shift leader position in the near future. I enjoy working here and would value the opportunity to stay and work toward a position with more responsibility.

To apply for Permanent Residency, I require a job title or job description on my Certificate of Employment related to supervisory, team leader, or shift leader positions.

It is possible that you may not be able to promise anything definite at this moment. I wanted you to know how much I enjoy working for your business and ask that you keep me in mind should a position become available. I like to be organized and prepare for my immigration process ahead of time.

Thank you for your support and consideration. If I can provide you with any information, please let me know.

Best regards,

Gus Castro

Augustine Castro

THANK-YOU LETTERS

A "thank you" letter is just a little thing, but it can be the difference between getting the job and not! Most candidates don't acknowledge the time the interviewer takes to talk to them. Yet, the thank you letter demonstrates your appreciation to your potential employer for their time and validates your enthusiasm for the position. It is important to mail or email the thank you letter on the day of the interview and certainly within 24 hours of the interview.

Some candidates take the time to hand-deliver the thank you note so they are "seen" again by the office staff. This is another way to be "recognized" and remembered. However, you can also be acknowledged using various methods, including a polite email, an attached MS Word document, a thank you card or a handwritten note.

> A thank you letter can distinguish between getting the job and not.

Benefits of Sending a Thank You Letter

You'll:

- **Stand out from the other applicants** because most people don't take the time to do this.

- **Make a good impression** by showing your interest and gratitude for their time, bringing up information they shared about the company, and expressing your increased interest.

- **Have another chance if you forgot to say what you should have said.** We often reflect and realize, "Oh my gosh, I should have said __." Bring up the topic and say you would like to *elaborate* or *expand*, or you *had time to think about this* and want to convey the following information.

- **Be able to explain further if your interviewer shared a concern.** If you were told the perfect candidate must have certain skills during the interview and your lack in one of these areas was a concern, you must discuss this again! Concisely bring it up, restate why this would not be a problem in that particular job (or how you would deal with it), and promote how, despite this "weakness," you see it as an area of growth, rather than a detriment. (Read the thank you letter in this book that addresses this issue).

- **Just want to say thank you.** Even if you believe your interview was flawless, you may not know how your competition performed, nor would you know what kind of thank you letter they prepared. So, in this case, thank them and mention your strengths again that would be useful to the organization to connect your qualifications that the employer expressed during the interview.

1234 South Bend Avenue
Kelowna, BC V1W 1X4
V7K 2L5

March 27, 202_

Mr. Charles Hansen
Production Manager
ABL Television Studio Ltd.
Ste. 2070-One West Monroe Street
Kelowna, BC V1W 1X3

Dear Mr. Hansen:

<u>RE: INTERNSHIP PROGRAM</u>

Thank you for meeting me to discuss the opportunity to intern with ABL Television in your Reporting Department. I thoroughly enjoyed meeting the staff and was impressed with the smooth coordination of tasks to execute an outstanding show.

After discussing the position, I am even more interested in joining you and your team. My education and experience gained through my internship college program in Media Production have prepared me to perform the duties involved in the internship you offer. I'm keen to learn and apply the skills from ABL.

I have attached copies of the references that you requested. Again, thank you for the interview, and I look forward to hearing from you shortly.

Sincerely,

Paul

Paul Gordien

Enclosure

Thank You Letters

The content is within the email and not as a separate document.

Dear Mr. Smithers:

I thoroughly enjoyed meeting you yesterday to discuss the opportunity to work in the E-Creative Graphics department. Not only did the position sound perfect for my skills, but I was also impressed with the company's values and vision.

Thank you for taking the time to introduce me to Henry, the department manager, and the other staff. The relaxed, friendly culture appealed to me, and I could see myself fitting in easily.

I am also very flexible regarding my time and availability. This will allow me to give the attention needed for projects with harsh deadlines.

I look forward to your call once you've made your final decision.

Yours truly,

Lyla

****

Dear Anya:

I thoroughly enjoyed the experience of talking with you and your project management team yesterday. What a dynamic group! The respect and energy you shared only increased my interest in joining you.

In the past, I've been told that my strengths in facilitating a team, keeping focused on the task, and respecting everyone's genius greatly benefit the team. It is my intention to prove my value should I be fortunate enough to be chosen for this position.

Have a wonderful day, Anya. Choose me! I'm ready to join you! Thanks again.

Yours truly,

Peter

Overcoming a "flaw" (emailed content)

Dear Samantha:

Thank you so much for taking the time to interview me yesterday afternoon. Knowing more about the job and the people has only increased my interest in this position.

I wanted to address your concern about my lack of knowledge of Canva Pro, as that was a key factor in choosing the best candidate. After our interview, I hired a Canva mentor for three hours and participated in some tutorials through Canva. I clearly understand the programs now and how to apply my knowledge in social media marketing. I am confident about using and practicing my new skills daily so that when you are ready to select your candidate, you may feel confident considering my application.

I have attached some of the work that I did today on Canva Pro to indicate what I have learned. I hope this will satisfy your concerns. I'll look forward to hearing from you soon.

Respectfully,

Monika

Acknowledging a Rejection Letter

Dear Mr. Wilshire:

Thank you for informing me that I was not selected for the graphic designer position. Although I am disappointed, I hope you will keep me in mind for future opportunities that may come along.

Please thank Chantelle, your assistant, for her input, and I look forward to keeping in touch.

Sincerely,

Rasheed Kaun

Letters Used to Decline a Job Offer

Dear Mr. MacDonald:

Thank you for offering me the [state the position] position. Unfortunately, I must decline your kind offer, as I have been presented with another opportunity which I have decided to accept.

I appreciate your time interviewing me and hope your chosen candidate will serve you well. Thank you.

Sincerely,

Your Name

Letters Used for Leaving a Job

When resigning from a job, it's important to write a professional and respectful resignation letter to leave a positive impression on your employer. You may need them as a reference in the future, and you certainly don't want to "burn any bridges." Here are some tips on what to include in your resignation letter:

1. **Gratitude**: Start your letter by expressing appreciation for the opportunities you've had while working for the company. This will show your employer that you valued your time with the company.

2. **Reason for leaving:** You don't have to explain why you're leaving, but it's a good idea to give a brief reason, such as pursuing a new opportunity or relocating.

3. **Notice period**: Let your employer know when your last day of work will be and how much notice you give them. Two weeks' notice is typically standard, but your employment contract may require a longer notice period.

4. **Offer to help:** If possible or appropriate, help with the transition or train your replacement. This shows that you're committed to leaving on good terms and want to ensure a smooth transition for your employer.

5. **Closing remarks:** End your letter positively, thanking your employer and colleagues for your time with them.

NOTE: Some employers may welcome you working until your leave; however, depending on the situation, your employer may ask you to leave immediately. Remember that when you resign, you are not entitled to receive termination pay, severance pay, or Employment Income because you are the one to end the working relationship. Always check the policies and procedures to see if you need to give a certain amount of notice before you resign from the company. If you are let go by the employer, the employee could receive the three payments stated above.

Here is an example of a resignation letter:

Your mailing address

Date

Inside address

Dear [Manager's Name]:

It is bittersweet to tell you that I am resigning from my position as [Job Title] at [Company Name]. My last day of work will be [Date], which will provide [Number of weeks] notice.

I am grateful for the opportunities and experiences I've had while working at [Company Name]. I've learned a great deal, and I am grateful for the support and guidance provided by my colleagues.

The reason for my resignation is [Brief explanation of the reason for leaving, e.g., "to pursue a new opportunity" or "to relocate"]. I am committed to ensuring a smooth transition and will be available to assist in any way I can during this process.

Please let me know how I can assist during my remaining time at the company. Thank you again for the opportunities and support you have provided me.

Sincerely,

[Your Name]

Chapter Eight

APPLICATION FORMS

Many companies do not use application forms but prefer to receive a résumé. However, an application form indicates how to complete the entire form. People who come unprepared without information, a pen, or documents and thus leave blank areas are typically not considered for a job. The employer will assume you won't be prepared to work if you are not prepared to apply properly.

PERSONAL DATA	
Name: **Yuhan Duncan** Address: **1234 Fifth Street** City: **North Vancouver, BC** Postal Code: **V7K 3M5** Phone: **604-903-0022** SIN: (available upon being hired)	Job Desired: **Barista** Available: Mon. Tues. Wed. Thurs. Fri. Sat. Sun Day x x x x x x Night x x x When can you start working? **immediately**
How long at the present address? **12 yrs.** Previous Address: **2 yrs.**	I was referred to this company by: School: ___ Walked in: ___ Other: _____
Are you legally entitled to serve alcohol? **Yes** Are you legally entitled to work in Canada? **Yes**	How did you hear about this job? Friend **X** Newspaper Ad ___ Agency ___ Employee: **Tom Black**
In case of emergency on job, whom should we contact? Name: **Mr. Bill Duncan** Address: **1234 Fifth Street Burnaby, BC** Phone: **604-684-1234**	Were you ever employed with La Restaurante before? ___ Yes ___ X_ No From : _____ to _____ Job _____
Interests: **Sales, customer service, problem solving, management** **Sports such as skiing, swimming, baseball, soccer.**	Have you relatives working for us? No : _x_ Yes: ___ Name _____
	Is there anything we should know about you that would prevent you from doing this job? **No**
	Are you bondable? **Yes**
EDUCATION	

Name of School	City	Course	Dates of Study	Did you Complete?
BCIT	Burnaby, BC	Sales & Marketing	20-- 20--	Yes
Wayburn College	North Vancouver	Arts	2018- 2020	Yes

PLEASE COMPLETE REVERSE SIDE

WORK HISTORY	
Employer: **ABC Ltd.** Address: **1234 Eighth Avenue, New Westminster, BC** Phone: **778-655-1255**	Position: **Sales Rep** Reason for leaving: **More challenge was needed** From: **04/18** to: **Present** Pay Rate: **$17.50/hr**
Employer: **THE HUDSON'S BAY** Address: **PARK ROYAL, West Vancouver** Phone: **604-9 80-1153**	Position: **cashier, customer service** Reason for leaving: **not enough hours** From: **10/17** to: **03/18** Pay Rate: **$15.65/hr**
Employer: **Seymour Golf Course** Address: **Seymour Blvd, North Vancouver** Phone: **604-929-4444**	Position: **Restaurant busser & Server** Reason for leaving: **occasional work** From: **06/16** to: **03/17** Pay Rate: **$13.75/hr**

Summarize information: I enjoy working with people. I would be more challenged in a busy environment dealing with increased customer service and team building.

TO BE COMPLETED WITH MANAGER

Job Class: _____ Rate: _____   New Hire: _____ Vacation notice _____

Payroll # _____   Re Hire: _____ Termination _____

Start Date: _____ Start Date: _____   Change _____

Screener: _____
Comments: _____

First Interviewer: _____
Comments: _____

Final Interviewer: _____
Comments: _____

LA RESTAURANTE'S EMPLOYEE POLICY

<u>Drinking and Drugs</u>: At no time before or during a shift is it permissible for employees to consume or be under the Influence of alcoholic beverages within this unit. The use of illegal drugs under all of the above conditions is al forbidden. Disobeying these policies is cause for dismissal.

<u>Timeliness/lateness</u>: One "no show" for a scheduled shift without a sufficient reason is grounds for termination. Habitual lateness is grounds for termination.

Signature of employee	Signature of Manager

Chapter Nine

DROPPING OFF YOUR RÉSUMÉ IN PERSON

Step-by-Step

Before you set out with a folder full of résumés and general introduction letters, do a job search on Indeed.com, Glassdoor.com, or SimplyHired.com to see what types of companies are searching for applicants for the jobs you are interested in. Another option is to visit the organization's website and look for open careers or jobs. Typically, these would be the best places to begin. However, some people would rather go to a mall or location near their homes or university and drop off their résumé. This section discusses all these options.

Although many businesses advertise online, the majority don't. Instead, they network and tell their friends and employees to spread the word or hang a "help wanted" sign in the window.

1. PREPARE. Print about a dozen "introduction" letters and résumés to hand out. Staple the letter to the résumé. Dress as if you were going to be interviewed during your visit because that can happen. Take a dual-pocket folder to place your résumés and a paper pad for notes.

2. PLAN. Don't waste time zigzagging your business stops all through your town. Choose a street, mall, or territory and go. 'Just Do It,' as Nike would say. Have a written list of the businesses you are visiting. If you drop in and don't write

their business information down, then get their business card with their essential contact info. Write a note on the card to indicate the date you dropped by with your résumé.

3. BREATHE. The first time is always the hardest. Take several deep breaths before you approach the door. Once you've completed one résumé conversation, the rest is more straightforward and much easier.

4. ENTER. Take a big breath again. Approach someone who looks like they might be in charge. Ask them: "Is the manager in?" They might ask what it's about, and you can say, "I'd like to apply for work and would like to offer my résumé and tell them a bit about myself."

5. OFFER THE RÉSUMÉ. You will be directed to the manager or a staff member who will take your résumé. Say something like, "I'm seeking part-time (full-time) work. I would like you to accept my résumé and consider me for your company (store, organization, recreation center, etc.). If they seem interested, you can continue. "I am looking for a position where I can (describe what you'd like to do, based on your experience or your strengths and skills) and am ready to work 20 hours or more each week while I attend university." Then...let them talk. They might ask what kind of work you are looking for. If you've never had a job or developed working skills, you can say something like this: "I've not had much experience, but I am keen to work behind the scenes, stocking shelves, working in the warehouse, bagging, or helping customers. I want to learn more about

working in Canada and am someone you can count on. I'm organized and like to keep a tidy environment."

6. "NO, THANK YOU." Bummer! If they are not hiring in the next month, thank them for their time, and ask: "Would you know of any of your associates who might be looking for someone in their organization?" You never know, as most jobs are never advertised, and often jobs are based on word of mouth from others. Thank them if you get a lead, and write the info down in your contact sheet or notebook.

7. "WHEN CAN YOU START?" Hopefully, this question comes after a proper interview. Understand that some small business owners are not trained in interview skills and may glance at your résumé without finding out much about you or telling you much about your responsibilities. Beware! It would be best to ask questions about the job, the tasks, the hours, and the company. Prepare for the question, "When can you start?" Know the days/nights you can work. You can start by saying, "I can work evenings and weekends beginning next week, and I can work 20 – 24 hours a week.

8. "GET BACK TO US." Chances are you might have to contact the manager again or go back. Ask for their business card and bend the corner of the card if a position looks promising. That way, you'll remember to record it as an important callback. Ask when the best time would be to contact or see them. Write it down on your record sheet, look them in the eye, smile, and say, "Thank you for your time.

9. BEFORE YOU LEAVE. "Thank you for your time. I look forward to talking to you soon (on Tuesday, etc.)." Shake hands and say goodbye. Write the information down in your book or the sheet like the one on the next page.

10. ON TO THE NEXT BUSINESS and Repeat steps 4-9.

Sample Résumé Drop-Off Record

Monday	Company	Spoke to:	Left Résumé?	Results/Call back
E.G., 10:00	Royal Bank Hastings and Howe	John Doe, Customer Service Mgr.	Yes	Call Back Thursday 780-987-2424
10:00				
10:30				
11:00				
11:30				
1:00				
2:00				
3:00				
Tuesday				
10:00				
10:30				
11:00				
11:30				
1:00				
2:00				
3:00				
Wednesday				
10:00				
10:30				
11:00				
11:30				
1:00				
2:00				
3:00				
Thursday				
10:00				
10:30				
11:00				
11:30				
1:00				
2:00				
3:00				
Friday				
10:00				
10:30				
11:00				
11:30				
1:00				
2:00				
3:00				

Chapter Ten

WOO HOO! YOU'VE GOT AN INTERVIEW!

The Facts

The PURPOSE of the interview is a meeting between an employer and a job applicant to assess the applicant's suitability for a position within the organization. The employer and the applicant both have the right and the ability to accept or reject an offer. As the applicant, you seek a job that will use your strengths and skills and align with the company's core values, vision, and purpose. In reality, you are both "interviewing" each other to see if there is a perfect fit for the job, company culture and qualifications.

Let's Get Real About Interviews

Based on my survey results from over 500 new arrivals to Canada, over 90% of the respondents stated they feared being interviewed. You're not alone, as the majority of applicants are not prepared. Most stated they didn't know what to say or didn't know what type of job they wanted. This is all fixable. Others noted that their accent would be a barrier to communicating properly (and we covered how to improve your English earlier). Improving your English is a goal that will help you get a job and work in your new country. The one fear that surprised me was the *fear of rejection*. I firmly believe that if we wish to live our lives in fear, then that will be the life we live. Instead, switch your thinking or mindset to the fact that interviews are a way of gaining confidence, practicing the skill, and a "game" of numbers. You will be the one who has the power to accept or reject the job!

After a short while, you will eventually be so good at talking about yourself and applying your interview skills during each interview that you will only choose jobs that excite you.

It's like trying on a jacket in a store. You'll likely try on several sizes, styles, and colours at various prices. After you've rejected the ones that aren't a good fit, you'll find one that is a perfect fit. It is the same with a job. You will be "testing" the interviewer by asking important questions and learning more about the company culture, the people who work there, the leadership, and the job itself. Even if you feel pressured to get a job as quickly as possible to pay your bills, if it's not a good match, you'll leave the job after a few weeks and have to start all over again.

To avoid rejection, you need to do the work and prepare. That means writing the answers to various interview questions listed in this book and practicing them out loud until you know them so well that they will become a natural response. The ONLY reasons you will not do well at an interview are because you:

a. are not qualified for the job

b. don't communicate your answers well, and

c. haven't practiced or prepared yourself for the questions being asked.

Only _you_ are in control of how well you do. If you want something badly enough, you need to do the work. The same goes for people who have lived in this country all their lives.

As you've read, most employers do not respond to your online applications, which is frustrating. Some organizations send an auto-response to say they received your application, but only those considered for interviews will be contacted. This is due to the large number of applicants applying for jobs. Recruiters need to be efficient. Another thing to consider is that some companies will hire from within their company but are obliged to advertise the job even if they have someone in mind. They will not advertise that they are likely to hire someone who already works for them, even though you've gone through the process to apply. Continue job searching and apply to at least ten to twenty jobs weekly. If you have the time, people searching for work and having the time to explore will submit at least 10 to 25 plus résumés daily! Remember, it is a game of numbers. Eventually, you will find the best one for you!

When you are notified that you have been chosen to be interviewed, you will begin with one of several interviews, depending on the seniority of the position. Entry-level jobs may have one or two brief interviews, but others may have up to five. Below are the various types of interviews you can expect.

Types of Interviews:

- Initial phone or online interview
- Second Interview
- Panel Interview
- Short-list Interview

Preparation

Here's a checklist to be prepared for your first interview.

- ❑ Review the company's website to learn what they do, whom they serve and their vision and values.
- ❑ Read the interviewer's profile on LinkedIn.com. You can also do a name search on Google.
- ❑ Practice answering the interview questions at least ten times in front of the mirror.
- ❑ Re-write your interview question answers, if needed.
- ❑ Review your StrengthsFinder Assessment and highlight the phrases you find important.
- ❑ Make sure you've written personal examples for each of the five strengths.
- ❑ Choose the clothes you will wear for your (Zoom) interview.
- ❑ Set up the lights, camera, computer, chair and table for your interview.
- ❑ Make sure your eyes are looking at the camera and that you can be seen from the chest up in the camera.
- ❑ Set a glass of water within reach in case you are thirsty.
- ❑ Breathe.

Stage One

Your first interview is often with one person only (from the Human Resources department or a business manager/owner). It is usually via phone or virtually (Zoom, Microsoft Teams, WhatsApp). Depending on the interviewer, this first interview may only take 15 – 45 minutes.

If they are interested, your interviewer may eventually put you on a "shortlist" of three to five candidates and invite you back for a second or third interview. This may take time, as they will be interviewing others. Keep applying for jobs while you wait to hear back from employers.

Kinds of Interviews

1. <u>Online</u>: This is often the initial interview, where the questions are general, and they are getting to know you, your strengths, skills, and experience. The interviewer will discuss the job, the responsibilities and the organization. It is an interview, so you must be prepared for a formal interview if it is online. There's more about this method later.

2. <u>Structured</u>: Formal and organized. The setting is often in their office, and they will have a list of prepared questions and will usually take notes while you answer them.

3. <u>Unstructured</u>: The interviewer may have a relaxed, conversational approach, and the setting may be away from the office, such as a coffee shop or conference room.

4. <u>Lunch</u>: An interview over lunch can indicate significant interest in you as a candidate. Manners and eating etiquette count! (Hint!

Don't order soup, spaghetti, or messy foods – no slurping allowed, as that is considered poor etiquette).

5. <u>Panel</u>: Several people (three to twelve) will interview you during your interview time. The people will represent the managers or decision-makers for this position. Eye contact with each interviewer is critical when the interview is in person. When someone asks you a question, start your eye contact with that person and smile while you begin your answer. As you continue to speak, move your head toward the next person, and have eye contact while you continue speaking. Continue that behaviour with each person in the room to keep them engaged. End up by looking at the person who began the question. Smile.

6. <u>Group</u>: Sometimes, a company will interview several applicants simultaneously so that you can hear each other's answers. However, it is not necessarily a popular way of interviewing. This kind of competition can make you sweat! Stay calm, be honest, and show them you know your strengths and how you can contribute to the company. **Knowing yourself is vital**.

7. <u>Short List Interviews</u>: If you have made the rounds to be one of three or four people who are seriously being considered for the job, you will be on the "short list." Often the interviewer will be the intended manager of the department where you will work. They will ask you a series of questions related to the job and how you would handle certain challenges as an employee.

8. <u>Testing</u>: You may be asked to take skill or written tests. (e.g., typing, math, English, etc.). Today's standard speed for a position that involves a lot of typing is 60 to 90 words per minute. Even

if you type with only two fingers, your maximum speed might only be 40 wpm; however, that is not employable in a job that involves a lot of transcription, reports, or data entry. Use all fingers and practice increasing your speed for maximum speed. There are typing programs online for you to learn the proper fingering for the keyboard and to practice increasing your speed (E.g., www.typingclub.com).

Online or Phone Interviews

Online:

When you are offered an interview, you will be emailed a Zoom link (or Microsoft Teams link) and the time of your interview. Ensure you are familiar with the software being used for your interview. Having problems during the interview won't look good for your success. You will need a laptop or computer with video and sound. Apple computers have built-in cameras and speakers, but other computers or tablets require an attached camera and a speaker that can be accessed through a headset or earbuds connected through Bluetooth.

Setting up your computer for an interview is important. You must be in a quiet space with a tidy background. Your interviewer does not want to see your unmade bed or cluttered kitchen! Set the computer on a table with a relatively blank wall as a background, and ensure your head and chest are visible on the screen. You can test this by logging into your free Zoom account to see what everything looks like. You can use the light from a large window, or I use two small lamps on either side of my computer. Some people will purchase special "O" lights, but they are not usually effective unless they are large. To raise your computer to view your entire face and chest, you can prop your computer up on books or an ironing board if you have one. The main thing is that the interviewer needs to see a fully visible face, well-lit, so they can read your body language as you answer their questions.

They will tell you about the job, the hours, the tasks, and the company. They will ask general questions to learn more about your strengths, why you are interested in this job and how you think you can contribute to the organization. You are welcome to take notes, but let the interviewer know you will be taking notes, especially if you divert your eyes from the camera.

> When searching for the meaning of a word on an online dictionary, you will also have an option to listen to how the word is pronounced.

Smiling and having eye contact with your interviewer will show your personality and interest in the job. If you are nervous or typically shy, you may find this uncomfortable. Practice answering the interview questions in the mirror, and ensure you practice eye contact and smiling until it becomes natural. Listening carefully is critical to fully understanding what the interviewer is saying and asking. If you need them to clarify something, politely ask them to repeat the question. Speak slowly to pronounce your English words correctly. When a person is nervous, they typically speed up, and your communication may not be understood if you have a strong accent.

It is good to ask some questions, such as the job hours and the organization's goals for this job, and by all means, ask when they think they'll be able to decide on a candidate. Since you will continue your job search, you will want to know when they will decide on a candidate.

What if you are offered another job before you hear back from the original interviewer?

If you are offered another job in the meantime, and really want the job you were interviewed for, you can always contact this interviewer to let them know you've been offered a position. Let them know that if they were potentially going to offer you the job, you would prefer to accept theirs. It puts a little pressure on them to make a decision, and if you are not being considered, you can accept the second job offer. It is an important question, as waiting can be stressful. And, if they say they'll make a decision in two weeks, and you haven't heard by day 16, it's all right for you to call them and politely ask if they have made a decision for that position yet.

Interview Via the Phone

Most of the information above will apply when you have an interview by phone. Ensure you have your résumé and cover letter handy, as they may ask questions about the content. Have paper and pen available and your calendar in case they want to know when you can begin or plan for a second interview. You may not realize it, but your body language and smile are sensed over the phone. The listener can tell if you are enthusiastic about the job. Smiling, other gestures, agreeing, and leaning forward can positively impact your interview, even through the phone.

Checklist for In-Person Interviews

Preparation

- **Phone to confirm the interview and address.** Some businesses have multiple offices, and you don't want to go to the wrong location. Take a folder with you that contains the following:

- ❑ Three to four copies of your printed résumé (in case there is more than one interviewer)

- ❑ A reference sheet with at least three names/phone numbers and email addresses. (Make sure your references have approved you using their names).

- ❑ A small notebook and pen for notes

- ❑ A portfolio of sample work (often required for art or design fields)

- ❑ A list of questions you have prepared for the interviewer (Write one or two questions in big print on small 3"x5" index cards or a small notebook and lay them flat on your lap).

- **Research the company.** Before the interview, learn about the company on its website, the Internet, Glassdoor, or LinkedIn. Also, research the person who is performing the interview. You can Google their name or search for them on LinkedIn or the company website. It is very important for you to know about the company, what they do, whom they serve, and its values and vision. This knowledge will help you decide if this is a good match for you.

- **Dress appropriately.** Wear clothes that relate to the job you seek. If you are unsure, phone the receptionist or HR department and ask if there is a dress code at the office, as you are being interviewed for a job this week. You don't want to be overdressed or too casual compared to the interviewer and other employees.

Arrival

- **Go alone to the interview.** Do not bring friends or family members.

- **Determine your travel time.** Find out beforehand how long the trip from home to the interview will take. Check bus routes and parking locations. If you are driving, do a "dry run" to see how long it takes you and where parking is available. You can check Google Maps to determine the best route and approximate time to arrive at your destination. Typically, drive to the interview during the same time as your appointment. Traffic happens. You cannot be late for an interview.

- **Do not smoke (anything) or chew gum** before or during the interview.

- **Arrive 10-15 minutes before the interview.** Check your appearance in the washroom mirror. Remove your coat and hang it over your arm before entering the company or interview area.

- **Introduce yourself (by name) to the receptionist**, mention your appointment time and with whom, thank the person and wait quietly. If you are unsure how to pronounce your interviewer's name, ask the receptionist for clarity and say the name to yourself several times. Review your notes and questions while you wait.

- **Take a few minutes to relax and breathe.** Be friendly and businesslike with everyone. Remember, the interview begins when you walk in the door, as the interviewer may question the receptionist and other staff about your behaviour.

- **Turn your cell phone off.** Don't be tempted to look at your phone messages while you wait. Instead, observe the office and the interaction of the employees to get a sense of the culture.

During the Interview

- **Greet the interviewer by name** and introduce yourself; be ready to shake an offered hand.

- **Follow the interviewer's lead**, stay on topic, and ask for clarification where necessary. Provide copies of your résumé if needed or requested. Use eye contact, smile and sit up straight. Place your hands on your lap and try not to fidget. I recall a candidate who was so nervous that she peeled off her fingernails while answering the questions!

- **Provide specific facts and examples**, do not just answer with a "yes" or 'no."

- **Ask about a specific job** rather than appearing eager to do "anything." This may happen when you drop into a business without an appointment. That might mean you don't do anything well or are too eager to "settle."

- **Accentuate the positive.** If you're not great at a required skill, let him know you are willing to learn through training and look forward to improving your skill. (e.g., typing speed).

- **Be attentive to your body language**. Maintain eye contact, have good posture, keep your hands on your lap, smile, and sit comfortably.

- **Ask questions**. If you have any questions, refer to your notes (if necessary) and ask questions that have not already been covered. Ask for their business card before you leave, as you will need that information to send the thank you letter.

- **State your interest in the position** and organization with enthusiasm.

- **Remember to smile and breathe.** Speak clearly and loud enough for the interviewer to hear.

- **Nervous? Breathe and slow down your speech.** If you are concerned about your accent, slow down. That way, the listener will be able to understand you, and you will be able to enunciate your words clearly. Taking quiet slow breaths will help to calm your nerves.

- **Be alert for signs that the interview should end**. The recruiter may look at their watch or stop talking for a few seconds. Once the interview is over, leave promptly with a good-natured, courteous farewell. Shake hands and thank them for their time.

- **Say goodbye to the receptionist**. Remember, they often have input based on their first impression.

Afterwards

- **Write a thank you letter.** Email, mail, or deliver a thank you letter to the employer within 24 hours of your interview.

- **Follow-up.** Call back within a few days (or when they have indicated they will have completed interviewing) to see if they have decided.

- **Don't discuss money** or benefits until the job is offered to you.

Sample Interview

An excellent example of an interview can be found on YouTube: https://youtu.be/HG68Ymazo18

Chapter Eleven

DRESSING FOR INTERVIEW SUCCESS

Dress Better Than the Employees

Although there is a certain minimal level of professionalism in how we dress, interviewees must <u>exceed</u> these standards. Dress for the "next level" of the position you wish to have. For example, if your entry-level position requires you to wear a shirt and tie, wear a jacket or suit to the interview. Or, if the employees typically wear jeans or casual pants, wear pressed pants and a pressed shirt.

Create a Great First Impression

The correct image in an interview will give you a natural edge over your competition, and your appearance can strongly influence what you say! The key is to dress for your desired position, not the job you already have or are leaving. Play it safe.

Make certain your clothes are clean, pressed or free of wrinkles. Your hair should be clean and styled well. Don't wear a hat. Practice good hygiene with an antiperspirant, clean fingernails and clean or polished shoes. These details may seem insignificant to some people but may be a deciding factor for the interviewer. Below are more details on what is considered suitable.

> *If a candidate can't put themselves together professionally, why should the employer assume they can put it all together on the job?*
>
> *Unless you look the part, don't expect an offer.*

Ways of Checking the Dress Code Out First…

- Call or email your interview point of contact (HR Department receptionist) and ask about the company's dress code. You could ask: "How do people who work here usually dress?" or "What would you recommend I wear for an interview with this company?"

- Check the company's website and social media profiles for images of the people. You can often gain clues about the typical attire.

> **Nine out of ten of today's employers will reject an unsuitably dressed applicant without a second thought.**

- Visit the company's location (if convenient) and observe firsthand how employees dress.

- Do not ask your parents, friends, or associates for advice. They won't know.

- Ensure your clothes fit properly, all buttons close properly without tugging, all hems are intact, and the length of your pants or skirts is appropriate.

Guidelines in a Professional Setting (e.g., Banks, Law offices, Finance, Insurance)

Men

- Choose navy or grey suits or blazers, depending on the season. The darker the suit, the more authority it carries.

- Wear socks that complement the colour of the pants. Shoes should be laced and polished. (No sneakers, please).

- Pressed dress shirts should ideally be white, grey or blue and may have a thin stripe. The tie is a valuable accessory, so make your choice well to blend in with the shirt or jacket colour.

- Check how you look in a full-length mirror to ensure you look great!

- A navy blazer is always a good choice, as it pairs well with slacks in camel, beige, grey and navy.

- Men can pair a sweater or shirt with their jacket and forego a tie for a more casual look.

Women

- Women can choose a style and colour that is flattering to them. A dress, skirt and blouse, or slacks with a jacket are suitable for every interview. Fabrics matter, especially in a more formal setting. Do not choose anything see-through, flowy, or with a low-cut neckline. Ensure your clothes fit well without any pulling or constrictions.

- The length of the skirt should not be too short or too long. Check the current style for the people you work with, and choose a more conservative length. (Usually around the knee, give or take a few centimetres or inches).

- Ensure your nails are clean and filed; use a light polish if you wish. Wear make-up that is suitable for the daytime. A lip gloss on your lips and mascara or blush is often a nice touch if you are uncomfortable with make-up. Practice this look before you go to the interview. Please don't do a full make-up regime if you've never worn makeup before. You will definitely feel uncomfortable.

- Please select clean mid-heel or flat shoes; no open-toed shoes, sandals, flip flops, or stilettos.

- Choose conservative jewellery, and avoid anything that jingles, as it will distract the interviewer.

- Look in a full-length mirror before you leave your home.

Casual Employment Positions (e.g., Tech companies, start-ups)

- Men's business casual attire typically blends some formal and casual attire elements. It can include non-denim pants, blazers, button-down shirts and long-sleeved shirts with a pullover sweater.

- Blazers, jackets with dresses, pants or skirts that aren't part of a business suit are appropriate for women.

Creative Employment Environments (e.g., Fine art, design companies)

- You might find a more current dressing culture in companies such as design companies, art studios, or clothing boutiques. In this case, you might choose garments and accessories that reflect the latest trends and resemble the styles worn by their employees and clientele.

- For the interview, dress a step better than the employees. However, this is not your time to "outshine" the interviewer with your unique dressing style.

Are You Squeaky Clean?

Let's talk about hygiene

With North America being so diverse, knowing what is acceptable regarding regular hygiene is difficult. It's not a topic we like to discuss. But I have to address it, regardless.

In North America, most people shower or bathe at least daily. Depending on your activities, hair can be washed daily or every two days. Most also use an antiperspirant (not a deodorant) to stop perspiration from ruining their clothing and creating an odour that may be offensive to some people. Body odour occurs when our sweat mixes with bacteria and can stain our clothing, creating a permanent odour. We all have different bodies; some sweat, and others don't. Soaps, perfumes, or cologne will not mask a body odour, so an antiperspirant (not a deodorant) is advised. It has been noticed that even laundering our clothes will not necessarily erase the body odour and may spread throughout the garment. Sweaters are even worse at absorbing the invading scents. Although regular laundering will help, we must do the "nose" test before we wear an item to an interview or to work. Take a sniff under the arms of your garment. It must be cleaned if you can smell anything other than the natural fabric. Here's a suggestion for a simple, possible solution to eliminating body odour from your garments.

White vinegar *is a powerful odour neutralizer and works wonders on underarm areas of fabrics. Fill your washing machine with water, then add 1/3 cup of white* *vinegar. Turn off the machine and let the garment soak for 20 minutes, then launder as usual. If the item must be washed by hand, follow the same directions, then wash with laundry soap and rinse thoroughly. Lay flat or hang to dry, as needed.*

This was not an easy discussion for me. However, it has been an issue in my office in the past, and my employees complained. They had to set up desk fans to blow the offensive odour away from their noses. As a manager, I had the "delicate" task of discussing the issue with the offending employee. Vinegar and getting rid of one garment solved the problem.

The following tips are the hygiene basics for interviews and every work day.

Do

- Shave, shower, brush your teeth, clean your nails, and use an antiperspirant daily.

- Make sure your hair is clean, free of dandruff and in a style that is suitable for the position. Disregarding this area will negatively affect how you work at the company.

- Facial hair must be neat and groomed. Try to cover your tattoos during the interview.

- Use a little talcum powder, cornstarch, or antiperspirant if the palms of your hands sweat. Let them dry before you shake hands! Avoid using hand lotion as it tends to get sticky when nervous. (I learned that the hard way).

Avoid

- Using perfume, cologne or aftershave as some allergies may be affected

- A lot of accessories, especially things that dangle or make noise

- Wrinkled, torn, or inappropriate clothing

- Garments that feel uncomfortable, restrictive, or completely at odds with who you are

- A sleeveless top, unless under a jacket or cardigan

- An outfit that doesn't match the brand or culture of the company you want to work for (E.g., wearing khaki pants to a prestigious legal firm where everyone wears suits).

- A combination of completely different patterns, colours, textures

- Flip flops, athletic shoes, open-toed shoes or stilettos

- Jewelry that is oversized or makes noise or dangles, as the interviewer will be distracted

- The bling sparkly look with sequins or beading; wear conservative hosiery in neutral shades if needed

- A briefcase, a large water bottle, a backpack, or a handbag that does not demonstrate professionalism (E.g., a bag with anime images, cartoon characters, tassels, or sequins)

Some Great Places to Get a Free Outfit for Your Interview

Women

Dress for Success: This is an international, non-profit, fully sponsored organization where women can select one outfit, accessories, shoes and handbag for an interview…for free. Once you have a job, you can choose up to three outfits for work. All the items donated are in excellent condition and are available by appointment. There are many job-related services available through Dress for Success. (DressforSuccess.com)

Men

Working Gear: This is a warehouse of clothing and accessories for men, where you will be supplied with the appropriate clothing and accessories (e.g., ties, shoes) for an interview. Once you have found employment, you can choose the appropriate clothing for your new job, including steel-toed boots and other safety gear, if required. It is all free from donations and supportive organizations. They also have a barber shop for those who need a fresh new haircut or shave. (https://workinggear.ca) Although *Working Gear* is located in Vancouver, BC, each city has similar options that you can search on Google.

Other Places with Reduced Prices

Consignment Stores

These stores sell various clothing for women, men and children that previous owners have taken to these stores to be resold. When the items are sold, the store owner gives the original owner a percentage of the selling price. However, the buyer will pay well below the original price. Most neighbourhoods have a number of stores nearby. Although the clothes have been previously worn, all the clothes are current, cleaned professionally or washed and ironed and hung on hangers. They are also inspected for soiled spots, tears, missing buttons, and suitability for the current market. Many shops deal specifically for women, men, or children. Some stores cater to one demographic, and you may not often find one store that caters to all three.

I often brought in the items my children had outgrown, and with the money the store owed me from previous sales, I could outfit my children with new (to them) clothes. I often purchased outerwear for the children and myself and saved so much money. Each season, I was always amazed at the great items people got rid of that I could buy.

Church Bazaars

Many places of worship offer a "flea market" once or twice a year for the general public to purchase items for their homes. The money goes to support the church activities. People come with huge carrying bags to fill their homes with everything from Hallowe'en costumes, cutlery, paintings, fabric, furniture (indoor and outdoor), tools, clothing and accessories. I volunteer at our church's flea market, as we collect goods all year for a massive market in the fall. People come from next door to over 50 km away to get great deals. I've seen a family of four purchase winter coats, boots, hats, gloves, and sweaters for under $50. There are toys, books for all ages, technology, tools, furniture, clothing, fabric and an abundance of items that you can only imagine.

Thrift Store

The Salvation Army, Red Cross or hospitals often sponsor thrift stores. These stores also sell many pre-used items at low prices, where you can purchase two lamps, a toaster, dishes for four people, and a chair for under $100. Usually, there is no delivery, so you'll need a vehicle or a friend with a vehicle. Check to see if there is a "Thrift" store in your community.

Facebook Market or Craigslist

People advertise their items on these sites where you can purchase, negotiate, and pick up the items you want. Some items are free or have reduced prices, where you can find items ranging from pickle balls to automobiles.

Chapter Twelve

PUTTING IT ALL TOGETHER

Now that we have covered all the various pieces of the application (advertisement, cover letter and resume, it may be of value to show you how we can create an employment application taking into consideration the criteria of the job and how to emphasize your skills in your letter and resume that demonstrate you align with the employer's needs.

You'll first determine the key points in the advertisement, highlight them, and then paraphrase or use their words in your documents. Make certain you can validate these claims, as you be eliminated from the process if you are over-emphasizing your skills.

First is the Advertisement. You will note that the keywords in the following advertisement are highlighted. These phrases or terms must be added to your cover letter when describing your skills/strengths or résumé. You should not repeat the same skills in both documents.

Job details

Event Warehouse Manager
Salary: $55,000–$70,000 a year
Job type
Full-time, Permanent
Shift & schedule: Monday to Friday

About the Role:

We are looking for a strategic **Warehouse Manager** to oversee the operation of our rental warehouse facility in the Lower Mainland. As the Warehouse Manager, you will play a crucial role in leading and developing a warehouse team, ensuring that all equipment is properly prepared and delivered on time to our events, and you will collaborate with our production team to provide input on equipment needs and logistics planning to ensure high-quality event experiences for our clients. If you're a natural leader with a flair for warehouse management and live event production, apply today to put your mark on event experiences.

Who We Are:

SW Event Technology / Showtime Event & Display is a leading event services company in Canada, and our winning team of industry experts brings our client's dream events, both big and small, to life. We provide expert services to the nation's most exciting virtual, in-person and hybrid events ranging from concerts, sporting events, festivals, trade shows, and galas to conferences and equipment rentals. We deliver events far and wide across Canada.

What you will have the opportunity to do:

- Strategically manage and oversee the daily warehouse activities in compliance with the company's policies and vision
- Manage, organize, direct, and train a team of warehouse employees and establish, monitor, and manage operational goals
- Management and deployment of a fleet of vehicles
- Maintained the physical condition of the warehouse by planning and implementing new design layouts, inspecting equipment, and issuing work orders for repairs and requisitions for replacement.
- Monitor warehouse activities on incoming and outgoing inventory.
- Control and manage inventory levels by updating data in inventory software and conducting physical counts
- Manage equipment shortages and cross-rental allocations, coordinate cross-rental pickups and returns in conjunction with operations.
- Meet warehouse operational requirements by scheduling and assigning tasks to the warehouse team and following up on performance and results.

- Plans the workflow of the warehouse to optimize productivity and efficiency and provides recommendations for improvements to General Manager
- Uphold an effective warehouse team by selecting, orientating, training, coaching, motivating, and disciplining employees in conjunction with Human Resources practices.
- Maintain a safe and secure warehouse by establishing, following, and enforcing safety and security procedures and complying with legal regulations.
- Complete required administrative organization and record keeping, including inventory and maintenance logs
- Maintain a working knowledge of the equipment
- Other duties as required

To be successful in this role you:

- Have 3+ years of experience in managing a rental warehouse facility
- Experience in a high-velocity warehouse environment
- Have a solid understanding of audio, lighting, staging, video, and trade show equipment
- Extensive working knowledge of using an Inventory control management system
- Have a valid class 5 BC driver's license or equivalent
- Have experience driving large trucks and forklifts
- Are physically fit, safety-minded and able to lift 50+ lbs

Bonus Points if you have:

- Warehouse experience in the live events industry
- Degree/Diploma in Logistics or equivalent
- Experience using Flex Rental Solutions Inventory Management System

You might be the person we are looking for if you:

- Have a genuine interest in the events and entertainment industry
- Proven Leadership skills
- High initiative and self-motivation with a strong work ethic
- Ability to think critically and make sound decisions
- Excellent communication and presentation skills
- Ability to multi-task and manage time effectively
- Flexibility and adaptability to changing workloads
- Have excellent customer service skills
- Professional attitude and work ethic

A cover letter written for the previous advertisement:

DHAVIT AGARWAL
3456 52nd Street
Delta, BC V7K 4M0
p.singh05@outlook.com   788-556-1245

May 25, 202_

Mr. George McMasters, Manager
Complete Events 4 U
4587 72nd Avenue,
Delta, BC V78 4B6

Dear Mr. McMasters:

RE: Warehouse Manager Position

Seeing your offer for a warehouse manager for your events rental company created excitement as I meet most of the criteria you mentioned in your Indeed advertisement. Before settling in Vancouver, I left a similar position in Mumbai, India. I worked for a huge warehouse that equipped all movie sets and conferences with the equipment, tools, furniture, and technology needed. After four years as a worker there, I moved up to assistant manager, in charge of team management, inventory control and safety, and most administrative and customer service responsibilities. I moved to Vancouver three years ago and am eager to return to my love of making significant events happen through my seven years in this industry and two years working in a smaller events rental business in Canada.

As a recent graduate with a BA in Management in Vancouver, BC, I found that the courses where I excelled the most included organization development, systems thinking, critical thinking and human resources. I learned and applied my communication skills to engage, and motivate my team, was the leader of all my class teams, and developed more collaborative and time management skills. I am highly organized and detail-oriented and have always run a fluid inventory system for safety, quality and efficiency. I am highly motivated to work in this industry, as our results demonstrate the quality of our service, technology, and equipment to the client and all members of the crowd being served.

My attached resume will list the strengths and qualifications you require from the candidates. I am confident that I am not only qualified for this position but will come to you with experience, professionalism, a high work ethic, and the desire to remain in this industry.

I look forward to hearing from you to determine a suitable date to discuss my qualifications and your needs. Thank you for your time and for considering my application.

Yours truly,

Dhavit

Dhavit Agarwal

DHAVIT AGARWAL

3456 52nd Street
Delta, BC V7K 4M0
d.agarwal01@outlook.com   788-556-1245

PROFESSIONAL PROFILE

- Demonstrates leadership, dedication to quality, efficiency and team development for effective productivity and motivation
- Highly skilled in critical thinking, flexibility, solving problems, organization and taking initiative
- Exceptional communication and presentation skills, customer service, and professional work ethics
- Jujitsu champion in India and British Columbia; physically fit
- Knowledge and use of large trucks, forklifts, and other heavy-duty equipment
- Highly trained in technology, audio, lighting, and significant event preparation
- Fluent in English, Hindi and Gujarati

WORK EXPERIENCE

West Coast Events, Burnaby, BC   January 2021 - Present
Warehouse Worker
- Responsible for pulling all client orders for inventory, using the forklift to load the trucks, and delivering and unloading the equipment, furniture, lighting, etc., to the designated areas.
- Assisted the team in moving and setting up essential equipment at the destination. Communicated with event planners to ensure all items were delivered and correctly set up.

Mumbai Production Events Rentals, Mumbai, India   September 2018 – March 2020
Assistant Manager
- Fully responsible for organizing all inventory and collaborating with teams for efficiency
- Ensured the safety of all machinery and processes and that all equipment was in good repair
- Developed a desirable relationship with all team members and engaged them in motivation and goal-setting to provide outstanding ad effective customer service
- Created a time-efficient system that decreased loading and unloading time by 10%
- Organization, training, and goal achievement increased profits by 14% within nine months.

Mumbai Production Events Rentals, Mumbai, India March 2014 – August 2018
Warehouse Worker
- Learned to locate inventory efficiently, saving time in inspecting and loading the vehicles properly
- Earned my Class 5 Licence to drive a five-ton truck for deliveries; learned to drive a forklift
- Cleared the trucks when they arrived back and cleaned and ensured inventory was sanitized and in good repair before re-stocking
- Maintained inventory lists for repairs, replacement, and loss

Stage Left Productions, Mumbai, India January 2010 – January 2011
Grip (Training on the job)
- Responsible for developing and building production sets and constructing the equipment that supported the cameras. Hung lights, built dolly tracks, rig camera cranes and performed general rigging duties.

EDUCATION

City U of Seattle, Vancouver, BC
BA in Management, Graduated with a 3.8 (GPA) May 2023

Capilano University, North Vancouver, BC
Grip Work for Digital Imaging and Film Program (Canadian refresher class) May 2021

IIT Bombay - Indian Institute of Technology, Mumbai, India
Graduated Electrical Engineering December 2013

INTERESTS

- Physical fitness, Jiujitsu competitions, soccer
- Travel, film production, management, solving problems, fixing or building things

Chapter Thirteen

HOW TO 'WOW' THEM WITH YOUR INTERVIEW SKILLS!

Prepare, practice and <u>know</u> your answers before you're asked.

Let's face it; you've now learned more about your strengths, skills, values, attributes, best behaviours and unique talents. They are currently written down in the form of a résumé and letter. You've researched the jobs that could use your attributes, so there are no excuses for not scoring highly on your interview. But…it can be nerve-wracking, and some of you will find that your tongue feels like it has grown a meter and wraps around your feet, and… you start to sweat and stammer. "Oh my gosh, what is happening to me?" you'll ask. Welcome to the club of first-timers.

Confidence comes from practicing your answers to questions you've anticipated. Keep in mind that they are looking for someone who fits the following criteria:

a. You have the needed skills, experience, attitude, and values they want

b. You can back up your experience with stories and examples

c. You demonstrate excellent listening and communication abilities

d. You have excellent eye contact and body language and are engaged in the conversation

   e. You are confident in your answers and know all about the company and the job

Typical Job Interview Questions

You will experience all kinds of interviewers. Some will glance at your résumé, ask when you can start and say, "See you tomorrow." At the same time, others will grill you like you're under investigation. These days, however, the interviews for entry-level jobs are more casual and may likely take about 15- 30 minutes. If you seek a higher-level position, you may find yourself in several interviews, starting with a 30-minute phone or virtual interview and eventually speaking to an executive panel for an hour or more.

The only way a candidate can come across as "smooth" and "confident" is to know themselves and be prepared to answer the interview questions. I know I'm starting to sound like a broken record, but being prepared is critical if you want to improve your confidence and succeed.

A student once asked me what was necessary to "have an "edge" (or to be a preferred candidate) in the job market. The answer was easy…know yourself so well that even you will be impressed! But that takes practice. Lots of practice. Before going out for an interview, I recommend you WRITE the answers to all or most of these questions. Then, correct them grammatically so that they are easy to say. Finally, practice them in front of a mirror, with a friend, a parent or your pet dog…whoever will listen. One of my clients had not had an interview in several years. They diligently wrote out their answers to 20 interview questions. I asked the interview questions while we were having a coffee or driving the car. After several practice times, my friend sailed through his interview and got a job offer.

Some companies still ask the basic questions below; however, recruiters or human resources will likely ask "behavioural" questions (on the next pages) that require more experience-based or action-oriented answers than just a "yes or no." Either way, you must be prepared for both.

Some Typical Questions for Interviews

1. Tell me about yourself.

2. Why did you choose to apply to our organization?

3. Describe your ideal job.

4. Tell me about your strengths and weaknesses.

5. Where do you want to be in five years? Ten years?

6. Do you plan to return to school for further education?

7. What skills have you developed?

8. Did you work while going to school? In what position?

9. What did you enjoy most about your last employment?

10. What did you enjoy least about your previous job?

As mentioned, recruiters ask deeper questions to determine what you would do in certain situations. They ask **Behavioural questions**.

Behavioural Interview Questions

Most jobs describe a person's expected skills, strengths, recognizable behaviours, and values. These relate to "competencies," the measurable or observable knowledge, skills, abilities, and behaviours critical to successful job performance. Based on a specific competency, behavioural interview questions are designed to assess how you have "behaved" or acted in certain scenarios or situations. These behaviours indicate how you might behave in the future within the role to which you are applying. It is essential to provide the interviewer with "evidence" of appropriate behaviour during the interview.

Behavioural interview questions usually start with the following:

- "Tell me about a time when you…"
- "Describe a time when you…"
- "Explain a situation you were in where you…"

As you can see, it is critical that you provide information that matches the criteria they are seeking. One way to do this is to use the **STAR** technique. The **STAR** technique is an acronym for remembering how to answer a question or scenario (Indeed, 2023).

S   **SITUATION**: Explain the position you were in.

T   **TASK**: Describe the task that needed to be completed.

A	**ACTION**:	Explain what action(s) you and others took to resolve the situation
R	**RESULT**:	Describe the outcome of your and others' actions.

TIP #1 – The most important thing to remember when preparing for any behavioural interview is to provide evidence matching the assessable competencies. For example, if you are asked a question about your ability to deliver excellent customer service, give a specific situation where you went above and beyond what was required to provide exceptional service. Interviewees who give in-depth, clear answers will score highly during behavioural interviews.

TIP #2 – The most effective way to answer any behavioural interview question is to utilize the STAR technique: Situation, Task, Action and Result. Add your reflection to indicate that you can continuously improve upon your reflection of your performance in any given situation.

TIP #3 – To get prepared for the behavioural questions, read the job description for the advertised position and look for specific competencies these want, such as 'able to work under pressure,' 'capable of delivering excellent customer service,' 'problem-solving and using initiative,' etc. These behaviours will be assessed at your interview.

Examples of Behavioural Interview Questions

Tell me about a problematic work challenge you had to overcome.

You can base your story on this type of answer:

"I was working on a time-sensitive project with three other team members. We were two months into the project when our manager decided she wanted us to start the project again from scratch while still sticking to the same timeframe for completion. Although disappointed, I put myself in her shoes and tried to understand why the project needed to change. I took the challenge and encouraged the other team members to do the same. We created a new action plan, considering the restricted timescale and moving forward positively. We recruited another team member to ensure the project was completed on time. The result was that we managed to complete the project on time, to the required standard and more importantly, to the satisfaction of my manager" (Indeed, 2023).

Why have you chosen this type of job over others?

- "I agree with your organization's sustainability values. This year, I gave myself a personal goal of using less plastic, and I want to do more."

- "I have loved increasing my technical skills over the last few years, but now I want to get back to leading people, which is exactly what this role offers."

- "I have focused on your company for a long time and noticed that you have significantly changed your long-term goals. You are well known for your exceptional culture, and I have been interested in your recent product launches. I would love to be able to contribute to your company's future."

Below are some typical Behaviour Questions to read and **prepare your answers**. I suggest you start by writing your script of what you will say. Practice reading your answers out loud. Once familiar with the content, you can rewrite your answers with phrases or prompts of examples, stories, or experiences.

Typical Behavioural Interview Questions

1. Give an example where you worked with other people to complete a difficult task.

2. Tell me about a stressful situation at work and how you handled it.

3. Describe a time when you delivered excellent customer care.

4. Tell me about a time when you disagreed with your supervisor on accomplishing something and how you handled it.

5. If your employer was struggling to meet a deadline with a project, tell me how you might go out of your way to help them.

> *You would be doing yourself a huge favour to write your answers to each of these questions.*
>
> *By far, this will help you feel more confident in being prepared for the ideal job you want.*

6. Give me an example of one of your goals and explain how you achieved it.

7. Tell me about a time your co-workers had a conflict. How did you handle it? Would you do anything different today?

8. Describe a time when you had to adapt to significant changes at work.

9. Give me an example of when you have met a tight deadline.

10. Describe a stressful work situation you were in and how you handled it.

Weaknesses …We All Have Them

Many interviewers ask about the candidate's weaknesses. Even though you may be hesitant to discuss your weaknesses, you can always spin a positive light on how you are aware of the weakness, what you have learned from it and what you are doing to improve or overcome the weak areas.

Below are some examples.

Tell me about your weaknesses:

- "I tend to focus too much on small details. However, it can add unnecessary work to my plate, though I have been able to catch mistakes this way. I am working on letting go of what's out of my control and reminding myself of the big picture."

- "I have trouble saying no. This can mean priorities get thrown out of order. I am working on this by having open discussions with my supervisor on what my focus should be at that moment to help me with time management."

- "I tend to get so wrapped up in a project that I lose track of my time. However, I now have a timer on my watch that keeps me focused on the task, and I am much more efficient and productive this way."

- I often get frustrated when a cohort is not accountable for their responsibilities. I have learned the value of saying something to that person to develop a viable solution.

Below, I've included some additional questions that I teach to Human Resource professionals and with an explanation of what they will look for in your answers.

1. How do you envision your ideal workweek?

HR managers can determine the work environment or team dynamics that will help you be most effective. They may ask how you've discovered and shared ways to collaborate on ideas or productivity with a team. The recruiter will determine if the answers sound compatible with the work styles of their team.

2. Tell me how you have used your problem-solving skills and leadership in school, work, clubs or past activities.

Even if your skills aren't an exact match for what you'll be doing at the company, you can tell a brief story with a clear point where those problem-solving skills will be useful when encountering various challenges in your new role.

3. Explain why you're choosing this line of work.

Your answer should give the recruiter an idea if there's a fit between the company's and your values. Prepare your answers as they may also ask, "If you had to convince a friend or colleague to apply for this job, what might you tell them?" Or "What keeps you coming to work besides the paycheque?"

4. What would you do if you got behind schedule on your portion of a project?

Your answer will indicate your time management and problem-solving skills and how you'd seek advice or assistance to complete a task on time. Some people may sacrifice their time or health to finish the project; when they could have asked for help or delegated part of the project to others.

5. What would you do if you met with a senior leader and an important phone call you were expecting came through?

This is not the time to take a call unless it's a family emergency. If you expect news of great importance (e.g., your mother was in surgery, and the doctor is calling), let your manager know *before* the meeting begins. Otherwise, put your phone on silent mode. This scenario will lend insight into how you handle completing your priorities when you can't or should not do two things simultaneously. No multi-tasking here.

6. Give me an example of when you worked in a diverse group with different opinions.

It would be a red flag if you did not have inclusive behaviour and collaboration examples. Diversity and getting along with people from other countries is a necessity.

7. Tell me about the volunteer or charity work you do.

We expect that your generation is passionate about giving back through local charities, missionary work, or service. Do you resonate with the organization's values or purpose? Giving and selflessness are hallmarks of great leaders.

8. Tell me about a large project you worked on – and your role – that took longer to complete than planned.

Since generations Z and Y (Millennials) grew up with constant stimulation, they can be seen as impatient. How a person reacts when something takes longer than expected is essential to the recruiter.

9. Would you rather work at home, in a traditional office, or in an office with an open floor plan?

Young people have preferences for how to work, and you will want to ask the employer what they offer before you state your choice. Flexibility is an essential benefit for youth and the company for high productivity.

10. How do you like to receive feedback?

Requiring feedback is not only to ensure you're doing the job correctly. Employers vary in opinion about giving positive feedback; many believe it is unnecessary if employees handle their responsibilities well. Some younger generations still need continuing validation that they are doing a good job, while others only need a "thank you." State what you need in the way of feedback.

If you give feedback to your supervisor or a work colleague, one of the best methods is the *Sandwich Method*.

State:

1. what was done well (the slice of bread)

2. what can still improve (the insides of the sandwich)

3. add a positive comment (the other slice of bread)

It might sound like this: "I really want to congratulate you on your excellent report, Henry. Before you submit it to the committee, you can add a section comparing the budget and actual expenditures. Once you complete that portion, your report will be extremely informative for the team."

11. Tell me about when things felt helpless, but you knew you would pull through.

Prepare an example of this, how you managed the situation, and then end on a positive note. Companies hire people with optimism, and you will find they reach for big goals and try to change the future for the better.

12. What role do you expect to have in three to five years?

This question may sound overconfident, but if you have a strong desire for achievement and promotion, which is realistic, let them know. Many employers are shocked that candidates' responses are loftier than possible. Please don't say you want their job in five years. I tried that once when I was young, over-confident and ignorant about their job responsibilities and the hard work it took for them to get there. By the way, I didn't get hired.

13. Tell me about when you were passed up for an award or promotion you felt you deserved.

Younger generations can get frustrated if they don't achieve or receive recognition regularly. How you respond to this question will give the employer an idea of your commitment and resiliency.

14. Imagine we've just hired you. What's the most important thing on your to-do list on the first day of work?"

Your answer will give the employer a sense of your organization, prioritization, judgment and decision-making skills. Think about how you will answer this question. Some ideas might include discussing with your supervisor their six-month goals for you in this position, learning more about the protocols and procedures, and finding out who is in the department and who might be a good "buddy" to help you with questions.

15. Let's discuss our organization. What do you want to know about us?

This statement suggests an open dialogue and establishes how curious and knowledgeable a candidate is about the company. If you don't ask questions about the job or the business, it's a safe bet your heart isn't in it. Employers listen for insightful questions that could demonstrate a sophisticated understanding of the circumstances of the job, the company, the competitive landscape, or the industry. See some suggestions below.

Do You Have Any Questions?

Prepare some questions for your interviewer as it shows interest; remember, you are "interviewing" them too. If offered the job, ask enough questions to gain the necessary answers to make a sound decision. Some questions might include the following:

- "Can you tell me why the job is open? Was the last person promoted or let go, or is this a new position?"

- "What would you like me to accomplish in this job in the next six months?"

- "To whom do I report? Will I get the opportunity to meet them before the job begins?"

- "Is the job located here or somewhere else?"

- "What type of training is available?" Or, "What kind of training is required, and how long is it?"

- "After a while, what skills and attributes are most needed to advance in the company?"

- "What are the realistic chances for growth in the job"

- "What has been the company's growth pattern over the last five years? Is it profitable? How is the state of the economy affecting the company?"

- "What changes are planned in the company's goals in the next two to five years?"

- "How regularly do performance evaluations occur?"

- "What flexibility is there in hours, location of work, and benefits?"

- "What is the company's stance on developing employees' personal and professional development or training?"

- "When do you expect to make a decision for this position?"

- "Do you have an onboarding system in place?" (This would include training, signing papers for employment, supplying university transcripts, etc.)

SKILLS AND ATTITUDES MATCH

Strengths	Weaknesses
• Possible salary review after three months • Strong career path is evident • Salary is fair for my skills • Training is a part of Onboarding • Manager is positive • Leadership team is respected • Organization's values are aligned with mine • I'll be part of a networking opportunity • I get to use several of my strengths • An excellent compensation package	• I'll be the assistant manager for at least a year • Pay is okay, but I'm still struggling with my bills • I'm the only person from my country • I'm not very outgoing • If I don't do well, I'll be stuck in this job • I still need to pay for parking, which is expensive
Opportunities	**Threats**
• University courses will be paid for a new degree • I'll meet some new people and have a more social life • My manager is leaving in 10 months, and I might be able to have a more senior role	• If my manager isn't happy, I'll be gone after three months • There may be a new manager within 10 months and then I may have to build trust all over again.

Chapter Fourteen

SALARY NEGOTIATION

How to Convince Your New Boss That You Are Worth it

The salary and compensation package (including all benefits) should be left until you are offered a job. However, sometimes, the recruiter will ask you what salary are hoping for, even in the first interview. The best way to deal with that question is to be prepared by researching what this type of position pays. With the Internet, it is much easier to determine. You can check various sources to find what similar companies are paying. (e.g., Google: "What is the going wage rate for a project manager in Vancouver, BC?"). Be specific in the position and location, as rates differ from region to region.

When negotiating a higher salary as an international student, it's important to approach the conversation professionally and clearly understand your value and the company's needs. Here are some tips on what to say to negotiate a higher salary:

1. <u>Highlight your qualifications</u>: Remind your employer of your qualifications and skills that make you a valuable asset to the company. This can include any relevant work experience, language skills, or unique perspectives you bring as an international student.

2. <u>Research industry standards</u>: Research the average salary range for your position and industry. This will help you argue more about why you deserve a higher salary. (You can also

check www.payscale.com/salary, www.Glassdoor.com or ChatGPT for some ideas.)

3. <u>Emphasize your work ethic:</u> Demonstrate your commitment to the company by highlighting your work ethics, willingness to learn and grow, and dedication to achieving the company's goals.

4. <u>Be confident:</u> Approach the negotiation with confidence and a positive attitude. Show that you're committed to working for the company and that you're eager to contribute your skills and experience to help the company succeed.

5. <u>Be open to compromise:</u> Negotiation is a two-way street, so be willing to listen to your employer's needs and find a compromise that works for both parties.

Here is an example of what you could say:

"I'm excited about the opportunity to work for this company, and my skills and qualifications make me a valuable asset to the team. As an international student, I bring unique perspectives and language skills that can help the company succeed in a global market. Based on my research and qualifications, a fair (higher) salary would be appropriate for this role. I'm committed to working hard and contributing to the company's success, and I hope we can find a mutually beneficial agreement."

Remember that the salary is:

Very important to **you**, but it is **not a priority** to the interviewer.

Of concern to him/her is… "Are you worth it"? Will you make money for the company? Will you create more income for the company than I will pay you?"

Questions regarding salary (or benefits/vacations) should be at the end of the interview process.

Sometimes, the interviewer will ask, "What salary are you expecting?" you have some **options.**

If you know your required income, give a range of what would be acceptable. For example, you could mention that based on your research and the value you bring to the company, you'd be happy to start at a salary of $45,000 to $55,000 annually. Of course, you need to fill in the blanks regarding the amount. If you are looking at an hourly wage, then you could offer a range that meets your needs and qualifications. As a young candidate, I remember being offered a salary barely covering my rent and transportation. Since I wanted double the company's offer, I politely declined, and the interview ended. This could have been avoided if I had researched before the interview!

Some other statements might be appropriate.

"I look at this job as a promising opportunity. I would be willing to start at a rate you are comfortable with and prove myself worthy of an increase in six to nine months."

"Frankly, since this is my first job in this field, I don't know what salary to expect. What were you paying the previous person?"

"I was paid $__ at my previous job and would like to improve this amount, now that I have Canadian experience."

"I understand the job pays between $60,000 and $68,000/year, and I would be glad to start anywhere in this range."

"I understand the job pays between $62,000 and $75,000 a year. I don't know how I compare with the other applicants, but I believe my qualifications and experience place me at the mid to higher end of the scale, and of course, I assure you that I will earn it."

Be sure you know under what circumstances you can expect the salary to be raised. A few organizations may consider a small increase after your three-month probationary period. While other companies firmly believe that after you have proven yourself in a year, they may consider raising your salary. New recruits who expect a raise after six months and ask for a raise at that time will likely be passed over for promotions or raises. It will annoy your supervisor, so I recommend learning from the human resources department or even your manager (at least six months after your probationary period) what the policy is for working towards an increase in your pay or a position with more responsibility.

Compensation

The compensation package comprises your basic pay (in wages per hour or as a monthly salary) and benefits. Depending on the organization, you may receive vacation benefits or vacation pay in lieu of time off, medical and dental benefits, where the organization may pay all or a portion of the fees, possibly a pension, life insurance, Employment Assistance Programs (EAP) for counselling and mental health issues, maternity/paternity leave, bereavement, parking, bonuses, and other options. This package is worth a lot of additional money, as many smaller businesses and entrepreneurs don't offer anything, and you would have to cover these costs on your own.

When I was offered a starting salary as a new manager, the annual amount was significantly lower than my previous salary. I asked if any part of the compensation package was negotiable. Having young children at home with a nanny, I was given the opportunity to work at home one day a week with pay. I also asked if my salary could be increased with the next significant client contract. The answer was "yes." Within six months, I not only worked four days a week but made up the difference in salary plus a little more. If you remain silent, nothing will change.

A Word of Caution

If you are offered the job, it is in your best interest to include your understanding of the reply to the offer letter before you sign your letter of acknowledgement or acceptance. Employers leave jobs too, and their replacement may not feel obligated to commit to an agreement they did not make or lacks evidence in the files.

It is good advice to keep a weekly journal of your work achievements so that when the time comes for a discussion regarding a raise or performance appraisal, you have clearly documented what you have accomplished and can demonstrate your value rather than trying to remember.

Waiting for a "YES"

As stressful as it may be, you may have a few weeks after your interview before you hear back from the organization. The importance of asking when they think they'll be deciding on a candidate is to allow you to follow up if they are not getting back to you promptly. You should, of course, continue your job search, regardless.

If the "decision" day comes and goes, and you've not heard, wait two days. It is perfectly acceptable to email or phone your interviewer to enquire if they have made a decision for the position. Let them know you are still very interested in the position and will look forward to hearing from them. You can even say it would be appreciated if they let you know either way. For now, assume they are very busy, and even though it may be on their minds, they haven't made the time to contact you.

During Covid, I applied for an instructor's position at a local university. I was fortunate to be interviewed and was informed that the government and university's policies limited the number of instructors with a Master's degree. However, the director was very interested in my qualifications and asked that I contact him in three weeks to see how things were progressing. I put a reminder in my calendar and called him three weeks later. Nothing yet. Again, he asked me to call at the end of the month. I did, and still nothing. This went on for almost 11 months, during which I called or emailed him monthly, stating my continued keen interest in the job, and I finally received a call from the director with an offer to teach. I was (proudly) nicknamed the "Squeaky Wheel." (It is a saying that the *squeaky wheel gets oiled*, and in this case, my persistence paid off by contacting the director to let him know that I was still eager to work for him maintained his interest to hire me.

When the job is really important to you, persistence will pay off. This was the second time I practiced being a persistent squeaky wheel to get a specific job, and my tenacity won. The job at the university brought me back to a life of joy during a time of darkness (Covid), and I have never looked back.

What Happens if You Get a Job Offer While Waiting for an Answer Elsewhere?

This is an ideal situation, really. However, you need to be honest with yourself. Would you rate both jobs equally, or would you prefer the job that is still pending? This is not a time to say, 'I don't know.' Perhaps you can do a SWOT analysis. SWOT is an acronym for Strengths, Weaknesses, Opportunities and Threats. You can also consider it like a list of Pros and Cons. With SWOT, you can analyze both jobs. Below is an example.

Job #1

Strengths

- Possible salary review after three months
- Strong career path is evident
- Salary is fair for my skills
- Training is a part of Onboarding
- Manager is positive
- Leadership team is respected
- Organization's values are aligned with mine
- I'll be part of a networking opportunity
- I get to use several of my strengths
- An excellent compensation package

Weaknesses

- I'll be the assistant manager for at least a year
- Pay is okay, but I'm still struggling with my bills
- I'm the only person from my country
- I'm not very outgoing
- If I don't do well, I'll be stuck in this job
- I still need to pay for parking, which is expensive

Opportunities

- University courses will be paid for a new degree
- I'll meet some new people and have a more social life
- My manager is leaving in 10 months, and I might be able to have a more senior role

Threats

- If my manager isn't happy, I'll be gone after three months.
- There may be a new manager within 10 months and then I may have to build trust all over again

Afterwards, you can do a SWOT analysis for Job #2 and compare them to make an informed decision.

If you get an offer but prefer another job, here's what you can say.

> "Thank you. I am very grateful for this offer. Although I am very interested, may I give you my response by the end of the week?"

There is always the chance they will say, "Yes," or "We can give you until Wednesday."

Then... phone the company you'd prefer to work for and say something like this:

> "Hello, Ms. Jones. I know you are still deciding on the [blank] position; however, I have had an offer from another company. My preference is the job with you. Can you give me some indication if I am a strong candidate? (Pause)

If yes...

> "That is great news. When do you think you'll be making your final decision?"

Hopefully, it may speed up their process, especially if you are on their shortlist and they know you prefer to work for them. They may not want to take the chance of losing you. However, you have some options if it is still a week before they decide. You can take your chances, say no to the offer, wait, and hope. You can explain that the other company needs an answer by the end of the week and you are also in a difficult spot. Or, you can accept the original offer and let Ms. Jones know you have taken the other job. As I often say, you need to communicate honestly about the right choice for you. This is a negotiation. You don't want to beg for the job, as that is unprofessional; however, you can honestly say that you would be very grateful if they could make a decision before the end of the week.

Communication is Key

When you come to a new country, it is natural for you to be concerned about our culture. The best thing you can do is ask questions to learn. If you are unclear on what a person is saying and searching your phone for a translation isn't fast enough, pause the conversation politely. Apologize for interrupting, and ask if they can repeat or explain in a different way. We do not expect you to understand all the words we say, and in many cases, the recruiter may also be an immigrant with an accent. That is what makes our country so very interesting and diverse. In Canada, we welcome people from other countries, and most people are extremely kind to give you the time you need to adjust to our ways.

However, an employer may become anxious if you are not doing your job as expected. In fact, it may be due to the employer not training you enough or giving you tasks too quickly. Remind them that you are doing your best to learn the new responsibilities in English. Ask if they could speak slower, as it would help you to understand their directions and learn to do the job properly.

Listening is an important part of communication. When given instructions, listen for the meaning of the entire message. Then, paraphrase or rephrase the message in your own words to ensure there is a clear understanding. Write down your own understanding in a notebook as you learn new tasks and instructions. Ask questions for clarity. I offer the same advice to all new recruits, no matter where they are from.

Chapter Fifteen

FIRST DAY ON THE JOB

Act Confident, Feel Confident

As a first-day employee, you want to feel and appear happy, self-assured and secure in this new position. When you look and act confident, you <u>feel</u> confident.

Arrive at least 15 minutes early. Come prepared with a few pens, a journal, and other tools that you'll need at work. Dress appropriately for your position. You'll have a much better idea of what others wear during your final interviews.

Introducing yourself to new office co-workers is another way to build confidence. Step forward and extend your hand when you meet someone for the first time. Your handshake should be firm, and you should look the person in the eye as you speak.

Onboarding

Some of your first days may be spent onboarding if you haven't been called into Human Resources before your first day. Onboarding usually includes signing paperwork and helping you easily transition into your job. Ensure you have read all documents carefully and have someone clarify any misunderstandings before you sign any papers. That would include filling out forms and signing documents. You'll need your address, social insurance number (SIN), contacts for emergencies, and a voided bank check if your pay is to be directly deposited to your bank account. You will be guided and introduced to your department, supervisor and some staff. In some companies, they introduce you to the team, while others will only show you to your desk.

Ask if a "buddy" or mentor will help you get oriented to find the lunchroom, restrooms, and copy machines. Hopefully, you will already know when training will occur and who will be training or guiding you. Make certain you ask questions to clarify your understanding of the tasks and procedures of the company or department. Some smaller businesses may not provide formal training or procedures, but you are entitled to these. Ask, and you will usually receive. If you don't ask, the supervisor will assume you know what to do, and you may likely make mistakes. It is your responsibility to have clarity in your tasks and duties. You'll need to ask many questions and won't need to apologize for your language or newness to the country. Show your gratitude with your personality to learn, listen and openly communicate your honest feelings (nervousness, excitement, fear of making mistakes, happiness to be there).

To help with your nervousness. Breathe in through your nose with a count of five, hold your breath for a count of four, and exhale to a count of six. Repeat. Your nerves will calm down, and so will you.

Know Who's Who

You'll be more confident on your first day if you quickly learn to recognize the people you meet. Use a small notebook to record each person you'll be working with. Use association tricks to remember who's who — their name =>same as your best friend's name), glasses, hair colour, Bill Campbell => Campbell's soup. Your self-confidence will increase, and you will impress the people you work with. You can even draw a rough map of their location in the office or building.

Know What's What

Learning a new workplace's workday or shift routine is as important as learning the names of the people you'll be working with.

If there is no written schedule of daily activities available, ask your supervisor about priorities for the day. Showing interest in office routines and procedures indicates you are there to do a good day's work. At that time, ask about any topics that are unclear to you.

Be Polite and Have Good Manners

People often tease Canadians for being so polite. However, it is something that many take pride in. Since our population is so diverse (age, gender, nationality, customs, education, positions etc.), it is difficult for newcomers to figure out how to act with all the people they meet. I regard good manners in high esteem and raise an eyebrow if I hear someone speaking rudely to another or even getting into an elevator first if an elder is also waiting. The key is to offer respect, kindness, good manners, and a smile to the boss and all others, no matter their diversity.

Ask Questions

Each office/workplace operates differently. The only right way to tackle a project or task is to do it the way it's done in that office.

Being adaptable and asking questions are important elements in learning workplace styles. When you first meet with your supervisor, you might mention that you will be more successful in meeting workplace needs if you can ask questions before beginning new assignments. You might also ask if there's anyone to whom you can direct minor questions about procedures.

Many people learn differently, and training or being shown how to do things in your job may be confusing if you are taught differently than you learn. I recall when the vice president attempted to explain an office design for our new office. She explained verbally. However, I could not "picture" the design as a visual learner. I asked her to quickly sketch out the office design so that I could visualize what she was explaining. I fully understood what she was thinking when the drawing was mapped out. Most people are visual; however, others are auditory (listen or hear), and others are semantic (need to see the words written) or Kinesthetic (where the action is used). (e.g., Kinesthetic learners learn by doing and often build models and use manipulatives, such as Legos, beads, and coins, to learn best.) Determine the best way you learn and suggest your trainer offer you the information in the way that you learn. Returning the favour by speaking to others in their learning style will build trust, rapport and a better relationship.

Remember, asking questions to gain clarity <u>before</u> beginning a task often prevents the need for redoing it.

Be Safe

Work smart, work safely! Make sure you, and those around you, can do your jobs and not get hurt. No one else can look out for your safety as well as you can. If you are asked to do something at work that isn't safe, remember that you have the right to refuse. Always know how to use machinery before you begin. Locate the first aid kit or fire extinguisher closest to you in case of an emergency.

By law, employers must:

- provide a safe and healthful workplace

- train employees to be aware of potential dangers and make sure that, when required, employees are certified with safety training

- correct someone who is completing a task in a way that is not safe, and change the unsafe conditions

- ensure that personal protective equipment is available

- report and investigate all accidents and incidents

As an employee, you must:

- know and obey all health and safety regulations

- protect yourself, your co-workers, and members of the public who may be affected by your actions

- report unsafe acts and unsafe conditions to your employer or their superiors, being ignored

- use personal protective gear as required by the employer (e.g., safety boots, glasses, gloves)

- report any accident or illness right away to your employer

Never assume that your employer knows and meets all the labour standards. Ask questions, pay attention to health and safety within your workplace, and don't be afraid to speak up and make appropriate suggestions for change. Although it may be daunting to question an employer about a safety issue, no job is worth risking your life or a limb. A good employer who would question your rights to a safe work environment is not worth working for, no matter the pay rate.

There are several advocates for employees, especially if they believe you are not being treated fairly or safely. One source in British Columbia is WorksafeBC.com. If your workplace poses dangerous equipment or chemicals or requires you to lift or carry heavy containers, this is not a good safety measure and should be reported. I always suggest you discuss your concern with your manager first, and if there is no immediate response, then contact WorkSafe BC and report your concerns. You will find a list of other employee sites on my website (joannemarlow.com/employmentguide). All people have rights.

Preplanning for Your Workweek

Summary of some key points:

- Preplan your wardrobe for work to save time. Choose clothes which are suitable for your job and ensure any uniforms are laundered regularly. Plan your clothes the night before to ensure they fit, clean, are pressed, and all the buttons are sewn on.

- Bring a notebook and a couple of pens with you. You should take some notes as you learn.

- Ask for a workplace tour.

- Map out the workplace. Know the locations of the staff room, restrooms, and other areas you will need.

- Ask about workplace procedures—where do employees eat lunch, are there coffee or vending machines (if any)? Can you drink a beverage at your desk or only at designated locations during breaks?

- Arrive at your workplace early. Be ready to begin on time. Arriving at 8:35 with a coffee in your hand will only mean that you did not manage your time well to get to work at 8:30. It also indicates that if you had time to get a purchased coffee, you had time to get to work at the appropriate time. Be at your desk or station before your start time.

- Verify when to take breaks. You are entitled to a short break every four hours, and most places will offer a 30-60-minute break for lunch during a full day's work. Get back to your job at the correct time. Set your watch or smartphone to ring several minutes before you are due back. If you leave the building for something to eat, place your order on an App, pay for it, and then pick it up. You will save so much time not waiting in line.

As with so many other experiences, <u>practice</u> is your best instructor. The more first-day experiences you have, the easier they become. Be well-prepared, keep your eyes and ears open, and you'll be off to a great start!

Chapter Sixteen

BUILDING A CAREER PATH

Knowing and understanding a career path is critical, especially if you accept an interesting job. After a few months, there is nothing more disappointing than learning that there is no future at this company other than the job you are now doing. In the section on interview questions, it is always a good idea to ask where this job could lead within the company. Some jobs that may seem elementary to you initially may lead to a supervisory job, manager, or franchise owner.

Consider your end goal. Get involved in jobs that "relate" to your end goal or will offer you training to build your experience, soft and hard skills, and where you can gain confidence in your new location. Choose the courses in your education and training that will build your skills and teach you how to apply those new skills in your new workplace.

Try looking at a career path as a five-year goal. You may already have a lot of experience in your own country. However, learning how to use those skills in a different country is critical if you wish to grow and be in a position that will grow as you learn and apply your skills. The benefit of having previous experience is that you can bring a new perspective to problems you may be able to solve. You can catch on quickly to new ways of using your previous skills, and advancement may be faster.

Meanwhile, you can search for related jobs to your ideal career. If you were a <u>dentist</u> in your country and dentistry is your goal in your new country, there are many positions you can consider in a dental office. Dental receptionist, dental office manager, dental hygienist, dental assistant, and periodontic assistant. These jobs pay well over minimum wage, and in time, you can return to school to become the dentist or profession you desire. Immigration laws and professional rules for credibility in your new country vary, and the government is not always responsible for those rules. Professional associations and universities create the protocols, education, experience and grades to deem a person is ready to practice (e.g., law, medicine, engineering, educators, architecture, etc.).

Another example includes a career path in <u>project management</u>, which typically starts with obtaining a degree in a relevant field such as business, engineering, or computer science. After that, gaining experience in project management is essential. Entry-level positions may include roles such as project coordinator or assistant project manager.

After gaining experience, one can further pursue advanced certification programs such as Project Management Professional (PMP) certification offered by the Project Management Institute (PMI) to demonstrate their knowledge and expertise in the field. Obtaining these certifications can lead to opportunities for promotion and higher-level project management roles.

As one progresses in their career, a person may take on more complex and high-stakes projects, leading to higher levels of responsibility and a need for greater strategic thinking and leadership.

This can lead to positions such as senior project manager or program manager.

Ultimately, project managers can aspire to become executives, such as Chief Operating Officer (COO) or Chief Executive Officer (CEO), with extensive experience in project management providing a strong foundation for these leadership positions.

A career path in <u>retail management</u> might look something like this:

Obtain a degree in a relevant field such as business, marketing or retail management. Gaining experience through paid internships or entry-level retail jobs such as sales associates, cashiers, or stock clerks will also help you progress. This will help you understand a retail store's day-to-day operations and learn the basics of customer service in your new country.

Develop new skills, including communication, leadership, problem-solving, and critical thinking, which will be important for advancing to a management position.

Building a professional network is essential for career advancement. You can attend job fairs, join professional organizations (Chambers of Commerce, Toastmasters, entrepreneur or business groups), and stay connected with alumni from your university.

Before advancing to management or the desired position, you will likely start with an assistant or supervisory role. These jobs will give you experience in managing teams, inventory and budgets. Pursuing further education is often a company benefit, where they may pay for your training before or after completing your certification or degree.

This can lead to a more senior management position in the retail industry.

Another option is to travel and learn a broader perspective and understanding of the retail industry in a global context. It can also increase your skills in cross-cultural communication and leadership.

For an international student to progress in a retail company to management requires a combination of education, experience, skills, networking and ambition. With dedication and hard work, you can achieve your career goals no matter where you are from (including Canada or the USA).

Chapter Seventeen

NAVIGATING CAREER CHALLENGES

Throughout this book, we've covered a lot of material that I hope will help you. This chapter will cover several concerns that people like you have expressed. It will seem like there is no focus in this chapter, but believe me, there is. I hope to minimize your concerns about coming to a new country and all that it offers.

Building Confidence

Most of us, no matter where we are from or our age, lack confidence when we face something new. This is no different when you apply for a job and have an interview. Thoughts may enter your mind, such as "Will I be good enough? Will I be able to say the right words that will qualify me? Will they like me? Am I too old or too young? Will I be rejected?" It is a frightening prospect of being turned down.

I recall how defeated I felt when I left the education field and attempted to enter the business world. My only business experience was for a year and a half before I entered my first teaching job. Recruiters searched my résumé for any indication that I had been in the workforce, as they certainly didn't think an educator could also be a manager. I often thought they should try to "manage" five classes of 45 students daily, create curricula, entertain and engage the "teams," and spend their free time grading papers, offering feedback, counselling, meeting deadlines, and researching current and relevant materials. I had to really know my skills and strengths to be able to "sell" them on taking a risk with someone who could master the new position, even though I didn't have years of experience in the business field. In reality, my teaching career provided me with a lot more management and leadership skills than I realized.

Gaining confidence has one (well, maybe more than one) solution. And it boils down to knowing what you really want (such as coming to a new country for a strong reason) and then turning it into a **SMART Goal** with an action plan. If you're not familiar with the acronym SMART, it represents five parts that must be in a clearly defined goal.

Here's an example of a SMART Goal:

> By September 30, 2024, I will complete my Bachelor of Science in Civil Engineering at Waterloo University with a Grade Point Average of at least 3.6 (out of 4.0).

Below is a further explanation of what the letters in this acronym mean and how important they are in helping you define a clear goal and to reach it.

S – Specific: Your goal must be clear. In the goal above, the specific part would be "Complete a BSc in Civil Engineering at Waterloo University."

M – Measurable: you must determine how you will know you have reached the goal. In this case, the measurable part is to "attain at least a 3.6 GPA."

A – Attainable: Can you get a degree within that time? Are your study habits and previous marks good enough for you to gain a GPA of 3.6 in a new language?

R – <u>Realistic</u>: Is this goal realistic? If you are still learning English, and your math and physics skills are not yet proven, you may need to extend the completion date or change your goal to ensure it is realistic. Do you have enough savings to pay for your life as a university student in a new country?

T – <u>Timebound</u>: For all goals, there must be a deadline. In the example above, the time to complete the goal is "September 30, 2024". I certainly have had a deadline for writing this book! The date, I must be honest, has changed a few times, as "life" happens, but I am now close to being finished, and my new date is realistic. Same with your goal. You need to know when you are aiming for completion.

Excuses are a time thief.
Have a goal, accept responsibility, and take action!
~Dr. Steve Maraboli

Saying that you "want to improve your marks," "save money for your travel to America," or even "lose weight" are not achievable SMART goals. You need proof of a benchmark (where you start and end with a specific date to reach your goal). Your goal must have all the SMART components; otherwise, it is merely a wish or a dream. And then, **put each task on your calendar.** When your action steps are written on your calendar, like "appointments" or "tasks," your goal will become a reality, not just a "wish."

Action Steps

Once you have a clear SMART goal written, your next task is to create small actionable steps to achieve the goal. For example, if your goal is to save $10,000 in two years, your action steps might begin like this:

1. Determine how many months you have from now to the end of your goal. Divide the $10,000 by the number of months to determine how much money needs to be saved or raised toward your goal. (E.g., $10,000/24 months=$ 417/month). You will need to save $417 each month to reach your goal.

2. Create a budget to determine what you are currently earning and spending and how much you can save monthly. This would include any guaranteed loans or gifts of money from family, as well. You must also determine the real costs of what you must sacrifice (fewer dinners out, fewer purchases, holidays, etc.) in order to save money.

3. Open a bank account where the money will automatically be deposited, which is difficult to retrieve electronically. (Opening an account far away from home and without withdrawal options helped me save for a seven-month trip to Europe when I was 21 years of age.)

4. Review your current expenditures and determine which typical expenses can be reduced or eliminated.

5. Add at least two-thirds of that amount to your savings account. For example, if you plan to reduce your expenses by $150 monthly, I suggest you deposit at least $100 into your "goal" account.

6. Repeat those actions until you have reached your goal.

7. Give yourself a small reward every time you reach $1000. A special coffee, a night out, etc.

8. Plan a reward when you complete your goal.

Some of you may be wondering why a reward is recommended. You need to be recognized for reaching several landmarks to reach your goal. I remember being motivated to reach a big goal that took several months to achieve, with the reward of skydiving. Jumping out of a small plane from 10,000 feet (over 3 KM) above the earth was exhilarating. The key word is "motivated." A reward can be small...a special coffee, a walk through the woods, sitting on a log at the beach...or a special activity, like skydiving!

Pleasing Others Instead of Yourself

Many of my students worry about their success at university. There are many reasons. Many people I interviewed were concerned they might disappoint their parents. True, some parents are helping you by funding your education, and you may feel obligated to them. However, most parents want you to be happy and for you to do your best. So, if you are not putting in the effort and doing your best, your fear of failure or guilt may be real. And, aren't "you" in control of yourself? Certainly, it is not up to someone else how hard you work. Life, even in one's own country, can be challenging, and now that you are in a new country, it is measurably more difficult. I know you can do this. It truly depends on how you look at the challenges and handle problems. Managing your time to study, find a job, work, improve your English and communication, budget your money, and make friends can be overwhelming. All of these categories or tasks require skills. If you need to sharpen some of these skills, you could take a few minutes each day and learn from lessons from YouTube. Just by entering what you need to learn, such as *time management,* into YouTube, you can watch a short video and learn a new skill. Learning and taking action on what you've studied is key! And I can guarantee that your confidence will grow and your fears will diminish. Putting your parents first will eventually be replaced with putting yourself first. Ultimately, doing the work and succeeding will give you the rewards you deserve and much more confidence. And your worrying will diminish.

Shame, Embarrassment and Fear-based Barriers

We all have times when shame or fear overrides our common sense. Shame is a perception of who we "think" we are. However, it is not necessarily based on truth or facts. It may be based on what we "believe" others think of us, and all those little stories we believed as small children when our parents gave us that "look," scolded us, or when an adult or sibling made fun of us. As a little girl, I recall my big brother telling me I was adopted. Of course, he said that as a funny joke, but I didn't realize that then. However, he didn't know I was concerned that my parents had only a few photos of me as a baby, and I wondered if he was right. Many parents get busy with their other children and take fewer pictures of a new baby. When I was three years old, I had an experience I believed to be true. I thought my parents had given me away to a stranger. That stranger happened to be my grandfather, whom I had never met. While my mother was recovering from major surgery, my grandparents cared for my brother and me in Saskatchewan, a long train ride away. Not understanding the situation, I believed I had been adopted or wasn't good enough for my parents to love or keep me. I actually didn't learn the real truth until I was an adult. As a result, I grew up being an over-achiever to prove my worth. Our personalities and behaviours are often based on stories we believe…even if they may not be true.

Psychologists have determined that before most children turn seven, they have experienced something they deem as "traumatic" and has impacted their lives, behaviour, and work ethics. In reality, it could have been painful, such as war, poverty due to the economy, divorced parents, or as simple as the death of a pet goldfish. Unless this belief is removed through obtaining and understanding the true facts or having a counsellor or coach helping you, the results of what you "believe" can affect your behaviour for years or your entire life.

Some of us are self-conscious about how tall (or short) we are, our weight, our reading ability, our education, or our communication ability. Yet, I believe we were all born perfect, flawless and extraordinary. What happens in our lives often affects how we view ourselves, but it is only our perception. We can change that perception to see ourselves differently. We are amazing human beings who offer value to the people we know and the organizations where we work. Our perception is not necessarily built on truth. If you are suffering from shame or a belief stopping you from being your best self, please read a book to help or get help. There is no shame in being the incredible person you really are.

Introverts versus Extroverts

I want to address the fact that we are all different. That is a good thing. We all have value and purpose. Being different and unique is where we tend to fit in with others. Employers will hire people with different strengths to get the tasks done efficiently. If someone has a weakness, someone who is strong in that area will ideally fill the gap! All people want to be heard and recognized for their good work and ideas. Some people are the first to speak up, answer questions, and be the life of the party, while others are more reserved or quiet and may appear disengaged. This is not true but only a perception. All people are valuable, and their intentions are generally good. Some demonstrate their actions and energy differently. It's not right or wrong. It's just different.

Introverts: Typically, the people who tend to be quiet in a group are perceived as shy, unmotivated, or disinterested. However, this view couldn't be further from the truth. Introverts are quieter than extroverts because they get their energy to think, solve problems, listen and analyze conversations without discussing with others. Instead, they are incredible listeners. They need a quiet place to think and resolve problems peacefully. They can do this by hiking, running, biking, sitting at the beach, or doing activities that typically do not involve conversation. They can regenerate their energy independently and return to a team with their needed energy. Their biggest gift is that they listen, resolve quietly and then return to the team with viable solutions. Sometimes, they will still need to be invited to share their input, as they may hesitate to speak up independently.

Extroverts: Although extroverts are often talkative and thrive in a group setting, they gain energy and creative ideas by "talking" out loud. They tend to sort their thoughts vocally and often are sparked by a comment someone makes or an idea enters their mind, and a solution evolves. They also need to recover in a quiet space to organize their thoughts, but not necessarily to regain their energy. They are not necessarily a person who needs attention or needs to be the life of the party. Instead, they need people to bounce off ideas and generate new ones. They benefit from a good listener and colleague who both listens and ask questions. Extroverts often benefit from a business coach.

I hope you can see that introverts and extroverts "work" differently to function. Both are needed in an organization, classroom, or family. No one is wrong or better than the other; they are just different (and important).

The Value of Former Work Relevance in a New Country

I have touched on this topic in a previous chapter. In North America, the policies and procedures to work (for anyone) are set by the government, universities, and in some cases, professional associations or industries. Many of you will arrive in our country with degrees, professions, and skills that are needed here. However, in light of safety standards and professional policies, all people from North America and globally are vetted to ensure that the qualifications needed for jobs have met a certain accepted standard. You are certainly permitted to challenge courses and skills that you have to reduce your time at university or qualify for certain certificates or a degree in your new country. If you wish to continue in your former profession, realize that starting in a less challenging job may be where you start but not necessarily where you will end up. As change is slow, you may become frustrated with dealing with the government's "red tape" or procedures. However, I see some movement in immigration laws, especially in accepting and allowing newcomers to enter some professions more quickly. This is especially true in occupations where we are extremely short-staffed. In some Canadian provinces, there are government grants (gifts of money) for people who wish to enter specific careers, and the grant will cover a portion of their training.

You will need to prove that you are willing to do the work, learn the work ethics in your new country and smile, knowing that these less-skilled tasks won't be forever. You must build trust with your supervisor and show you are dependable and willing to do the work and learn more each month. It is very important to communicate your interest in continuing your career at the organization (if you enjoy the culture and vision) and let them know you want to understand the career path options in this industry or organization. Always have your updated résumé ready should there be a new position at that company or elsewhere. This is the same advice I give to all people. I have observed that newcomers are willing to work harder and are often more determined to do what is needed to succeed. Many North Americans stand, watch, and wonder why they aren't getting jobs. To be focused on your goal, one must have a purpose, a north star, and a burning desire. Then, the next critical step is to take ACTION.

Immigration laws change constantly, and I hope to keep up with the changes, which will be updated on my website: (joannemarlow.com/employmentguide).

Chapter Eighteen

WHAT I KNOW FOR CERTAIN…
YOU WILL BE SUCCESSFUL

As I started this book in Chapter One, I told you how much I admired you for all the sacrifices you are making to move to a new country with a new language and where everything is different. I will always be in awe of your determination to succeed, which signifies your dedication to your goals.

I have had the opportunity to live my purpose for decades to guide and help others reach levels beyond their expectations. I am never surprised when some of my university graduates have come to me with joy and tears as they tell me they have just been offered the job of their dreams. They have done the work and followed my guidelines.

All people struggled in some way. The journey can be challenging and hard. But there is light at the end of the tunnel. Once you reach your destination, you will applaud yourself for staying the course, doing the hard work and reaching your target. You may end up having several goals. I call them Plans A, B and C. All are acceptable, but we must realize that your first job may not be plan A. You may have to accept Plan B, work at it, and eventually, Plan A will return. You will be wiser, more experienced, and more confident.

I want to share a beautiful letter I recently received from one of my university's international graduates, as his ultimate Plan A was finally achieved. He didn't give up. He listened to my words of encouragement and belief. He replaced fear with confidence and was rewarded.

"I am excited to share some wonderful news with you - I have recently received a job offer from one of the largest mining companies in Canada! As I reflect on my journey toward this achievement, I am reminded of the invaluable guidance and support you provided me during our time together in class and during the interview process.

I am writing to express my sincere gratitude for the life-changing lessons you have taught me. Your commitment to helping your students succeed is commendable, and I feel fortunate to have had you as my professor. Your teachings have equipped me with the necessary tools and skills to prepare for the job search process, from developing a strong résumé to writing a compelling cover letter and effectively answering behavioural questions during interviews.

I am grateful for your unwavering support, patience, and kindness throughout my time here, which have been instrumental in my success. Your positive influence has left a lasting impact on me, and I will always cherish the valuable lessons and experiences I gained from your classes."

A. Mustafa, (2023)

This type of result is what I hope for you as you read through this book and decide to move to North America. Is it going to be easy? Not likely. Can you do it? I believe you can. My plan for this book and for you is to offer you more than just a book to read. Over time, not only will I supply links and current information, templates, and resources on my website, but I will offer short videos and instructions on topics that are important to many of you.

(joannemarlow.com/employmentguide)

I am truly honoured that you have read the book this far. Only **you** can take the first step now. You need to want your goal to happen for a cause that is bigger than yourself.

YOU ARE EXTRAORDINARY.

You may not know why I can say that without knowing you, but I do know that you are beyond incredible. I believe in you and hope you can feel my energy and positive wishes for you throughout this book. Bit by bit, as you go through this journey, you will begin to develop and recognize the skills and strengths that will help you succeed. When you look in the mirror, you will see a new reflection. A person with confidence, a person who is happy and has stability. It will be worth it all.

Determining your "Why" or purpose in life is like a bright light guiding you to your destination. Maybe your purpose is like the North Star. It will guide you. I know how weird that might sound, but life gets easier with a compass or a bright light. Let me guide you on your journey, and know on each page of this book that you are on my mind. I care about you. My purpose is to help you reach your ideal job and feel happy. You will never be alone.

The Author

JoAnne E. Marlow, MA

JoAnne Marlow is a professional speaker and business educator on "How to Attract, Hire and Retain Your Best Talent." She is an authority on career selection, preparation and job satisfaction for people of all ages and has been offering her knowledge for several decades as an educator and presenter. This is her tenth published book, with five international best-sellers and five articles on Leadership. Her latest book, "25 Powerful Strategies to Hire and Successfully Retain Millennials" (2017), has been a best-selling book in Canada and the USA (Human Resources category).

Manufactured by Amazon.ca
Bolton, ON